# Power and
# Politics
# in Project
# Management

# Power and Politics in Project Management

Jeffrey K. Pinto, Ph.D.

## Library of Congress Cataloging-in-Publication Data

Pinto, Jeffrey K.
    Power and politics in project management / Jeffrey K. Pinto
      p.      cm.
    Includes bibliographical references and index.
    ISBN: 1–880410–43–5
    1. Industrial project management.   2. Power (Social sciences)
    I. Title.
HD69.P75.P5497    1996
658.4'04--dc20                           96–13110
                                               CIP

### Book Team

*Editor-in-Chief*
James S. Pennypacker

| *Copyeditor/Production Coordinator* | *Associate Editor* |
|---|---|
| Mark S. Parker | Sandy Jenkins |
| *Graphic Designer* | *Publications Coordinator* |
| Michelle Triggs Owen | Bobby R. Hensley |

PMI books are available at special quantity discounts to use as premiums and sales promotions, or for use in corporate training programs. For more information, please write to the Business Manager, PMI Communications, 40 Colonial Square, Sylva, NC 28779. Or contact your local bookstore.

The paper used in this book complies with the Permanent Paper Standard issued by the National Information Standards Organization (Z39.48–1984).

10   9   8   7   6   5   4   3   2   1

# Contents

Portions of chapter one through eight were adapted from *Successful Project Managers: Leading Your Team to Success*, by J.K. Pinto and O.P. Pharbanda. 1995. New York: Van Nostrand Reinhold.

Portions of chapter nine were adapted from *Successful Information System Implementation*, by J.K. Pinto. 1994. Upper Darby, PA: PMI Publications.

# Power and Politics in Project Management

*Politics is the conduct of public affairs for private advantage.*
Ambrose Bierce
The Devil's Dictionary

## Preface

One of the truly fascinating aspects of our business environment is the role that power and political behavior play in organizations. Most of us tend to regard political activity with a sort of repugnance, finding the conduct of politics to be personally distasteful and organizationally damaging. There is an interesting paradox at work here. Experience demonstrates to both practitioners and neutral observers that, for better or for worse, for all our often-expressed personal disdain for the exercise of politics, we readily acknowledge this process is often one of the prime moving forces within any organization.

Political behavior, sometimes defined as any process by which individuals and groups seek, acquire, and maintain power, is pervasive in modern corporations. Examples include activities as significant as negotiating a multimillion-dollar commitment for a new project to as mundane as who will attain a corner office; as predatory as the willful attempt to derail another's career to benign as deciding the location of the annual office party. The underlying feature of each of these examples is that the processes by which we make decisions and seek power, the issues we deem "power laden," and the steps we take to maintain our position are often an emotionally charged sequence of events with important personal and corporate ramifications.

The field of project management is fraught with political processes for several reasons. In many companies project managers do not have a stable power base, neither high status nor overriding authority. They must learn to cultivate other methods of influence to secure resources from other departments necessary to attain project success. A closely related issue is that projects often exist outside of the traditional structure, relegating project managers to the role of supernumerary. Nearly all resources must be negotiated and bargained for. Finally, many project managers are not given the authority to conduct formal performance evaluations on project team subordinates, denying them an important base of hierarchical power. Without the authority to reward or punish, influence is the only tool available to change subordinate behavior. Consequently, project managers must learn important "human" skills such as bargaining, influence, conflict management, and negotiation.

Successful project managers know the importance of maintaining strong political ties throughout their organizations as a method for achieving project success. It is rare to find senior project managers who are not conversant in and knowledgeable of the importance of politics in effectively performing their jobs. Political behavior can either be a project manager's best friend or most remorseless foe. Whatever decision one comes to regarding the use of politics in the quest for project success, it cannot be ignored: Use politics or risk being used by politics.

The above dictum does not have to make the reader uncomfortable. No one would argue that project managers must become immersed in the brutal, self-serving side of corporate political life. There are many examples of predatory behavior, making most of us leery of being considered "politically adept." Nevertheless, project management and politics are inextricably linked. Successful project managers intuitively understand their job consists of more than simply being technically and managerially competent.

My research and consulting experience has found many companies will spend thousands of hours to plan and implement multimillion- or even multibillion-dollar investments, develop intricate plans and schedules, and form a cohesive team, only to have the project derailed by political processes. This is a pity, particularly in that the end result is often foreseeable early in the development of the project—usually a result of a project manager's refusal to acknowledge and cultivate political ties, both internal and with the client.

This book, *Power and Politics in Project Management*, is written to fill an important niche on the manager's bookshelf by presenting a practical discussion of the role of political behavior in project implementation. As the chapter titles indicate, it offers a pragmatic guide to project management politics and the lessons managers need to derive from its practice.

The approach is a combination of theory and practice. The first chapters of the book lay a foundation, using important guiding principles from research on power and political behavior to put project politics in its proper context. We need to be well grounded in some basic theory of politics, understand the goals of projects, and the constraints that project managers face. Once the key decision processes that often influence interdepartmental cooperation and conflict are understood, it's easy to see how pervasive political behavior is and how to take steps to minimize its potentially negative effect on projects. The last chapter of the book examines some specific arenas of politics: negotiation skills, conflict management, and general conclusions that can be drawn from the study of power and politics.

My intention is to help project managers do a better job of running their projects by teaching valuable lessons about the scope and magnitude of political behavior.

This book is the natural result of a series of conversations I have had with project managers and academics over the past years. Max Wideman, Dennis Slevin, and Sam Mantel have all served as terrific sources for ideas and encouragement in both conceptualizing and undertaking this project. Fran Webster, in particular, through his dual role as PMI Editor and a personal friend, has been a tremendous source of enthusiasm and support when this book was no more than a series of vague ideas in the back of my head. His criticisms were always on target and easy to bear (Faithful are the wounds of a friend. Prov. 27:6). I also appreciate the support of Jim Pennypacker and the PMI staff through all phases of this book's development. Lastly, to my wife Mary Beth, I offer, with the sincerest gratitude, another acknowledgment of her love and the fruit it continues to bear in my life.

## chapter 1

# Project Management and the Problem of Politics

Tim Robinson has a problem. Sitting at his desk after yet another in a seemingly endless round of project planning meetings, he is beginning to wonder if his project will ever get off the ground. Tim, a bright young engineer, two years out of graduate school, is excited about his job as a software engineer with a major computer manufacturer. He has worked on several project teams since he joined the firm, and less than three months ago was given his first project to manage. The project, an upgrade of a popular system integration program, was considered important but not overly difficult to manage. Now, reflecting on recent events, Tim is not sure if it is even possible to complete the upgrade.

Problems started almost immediately after Tim was assigned the task of running the project. He set up a series of meetings with senior managers to get their support for the project and commitment of their personnel to staff the team. Quickly it became clear that, while never being overtly hostile, the managers—by and large—viewed his project as intrusive and were reluctant to commit themselves or their resources to his goals.

Tim's frustrations were encapsulated in a recent conversation with a senior manager in the diagnostics department. Diagnostics, charged with debugging all program code, is integral to the success of the program upgrade. Sitting at his desk, reflecting back on his rather one-sided conversation with Ed, the diagnostics manager, Tim felt bewildered and angry by the messages he received.

Tim told Ed, "I have to get a firm commitment from you for two of your people before we can kick off the upgrade project. The preliminary schedule I sent you last week shows they will need to be available on more or less a full-time basis within a month of project start-up."

"Well, Tim, the problem is that you're doing this at a real busy time in my schedule," Ed replied. "I'm already running these people at 40-plus hours per week and we're already committed to a full slate of projects into the early part of the fiscal year."

"Ed, I appreciate your concerns," Tim said, "but the folks at the top want this project to move fast. You know if we don't meet the September launch window we lose any market advantage the upgrade could give us."

Ed, clearly becoming irritated, said he knew the schedule, thought it was totally unrealistic and made clear he wouldn't "give up two of his people on a full-time basis when (Tim) whistle(s) for them."

Trying to control his mounting frustration, Tim replied, "Look, Ed, I know you have your hands full, but if we don't get this project moving, top management is ..."

"Is what?," Ed interrupted. "You keep referring to top management. Who are you talking about? Who's backing this project?"

"Well, you know," Tim tried to explain, "upper management wants this upgrade on the market as fast as ..."

Again interrupting, and now laughing at him, Ed tells Tim, "That's what I thought. Listen, kid, my boss—who is a member of top management—wants me to run this department as efficiently as possible. That means keeping my people at work on their current duties. All I got from you is a memo announcing a new project. Which do you think is more important, a memo from a junior manager or daily calls from the vice president asking me how things are going in the department?"

"So are you saying that you won't cooperate with this project?" asked Tim, now angry and visibly shaken.

"Did I say that?" Ed said innocently. "Of course I'll cooperate with your project, but you'll get your people when I can release them, not when you have 'got to' have them."

After that exchange, Tim had similar conversations with just about every line manager needed to support his project with personnel and resources. Now, sitting at his desk, Tim shakes his head and wonders how his project will get done on time. More importantly, he wonders exactly what he did wrong to bring the project to this state.

Tim's problems are not isolated, nor are they unusual. At some point, almost every project manager has faced the same issues Tim is confronting. Recalcitrant managers, unclear lines of authority, tentative resource commitments, lukewarm upper management support, and hard lessons in negotiation are all characteristics of many project managers' daily lives. And while the "Eds" of this world typically are somewhat more euphemistic, the message is generally as abundantly clear as the above dialogue. Set in this all-too-familiar framework, it is a wonder that most projects ever get accomplished.

The challenges these project managers face is the byproduct of the power games and political processes that inhabit our organizations. Whether the company is large or small, public or private, direct evidence of constant, frequently stifling political behavior is overwhelming. Indeed, these political activities, not technical problems, are some of the most commonly cited causes for new project failure.

It is ironic that while project management theorists have sought for years to find new and better methods to improve the discipline, power and political behavior—one of the most pervasive and frequently pernicious elements impacting project implementation—has rarely been addressed. Even in the cases where it has been examined, the discussion is often so cursory or theory-driven it offers little in the way of useful advice for practicing project managers. Whatever our current level of understanding of power and politics in organizations, we must realize its presence is ubiquitous, its impact significant, and begin to address it as a necessary part of project management, learning to use it to our advantage increases the likelihood of success.

Before exploring the concepts of organizational power and political behavior, it is important to establish the baseline, or context, of project management in most organizations. In doing so, we will see that the project management function, by definition and constraints, is one of the most natural arenas for political activities within firms.

# Introduction to Some Important Terms and Concepts

In an increasingly interwoven and fast-paced corporate environment, projects are the "engines of growth" for most companies. Whether the company regularly employs project teams or creates them as ad hoc "skunkworks" to address immediate crises or market opportunities, the use of projects and cross-functional teams continues to proliferate. At every level of business we find teams of people working on projects, headed by a project manager. Indeed, the use of project management is now a worldwide phenomenon.

The substantial increase in the use of project teams is a mixed blessing for most companies. Research and anecdotal evidence demonstrate tremendous flexibility and improved time to market that project-based work allows modern corporations. However, many companies starting to use project teams for the first time are also discovering the accompanying constraints project-based work offers. Among these are: (1) structural—relating to the way project teams are established and exist vis-à-vis the traditional functional hierarchy; (2) technical—consisting of the determination that the organization possesses the necessary training and technology to efficiently run *their* projects; and (3) behavioral—suggesting that many project-related problems are the result of human interactions, often due to the newly created cross-functional teams, different operating philosophies and goals held across various departments and levels in companies.

# What is a Project?

Although impressive examples of projects abound, actually defining a project is sometimes not easy. The recently opened Eurotunnel (or "Chunnel"), the successful bid for the 1996 Summer Olympic Games by the city of Atlanta, the Great Pyramids of Giza, and the Panama Canal are all famous examples of projects. On a smaller scale, finishing a team project at school, writing a term paper, decorating the house for a Christmas party or a visit from family, or a weekly shopping trip to the grocery store are all projects that we engage in on a daily, almost routine, basis. While vastly different in form, time frame, and objectives to be accomplished, each of the above examples, whether great or modest, share some common properties that define the nature and character of most projects.

In order to be meaningful, we need to consider definitions that are general enough to include a range of organizational activities that comprise "project functions." At the same time, the definition should be narrow enough so that we are able to focus specifically on those organizational activities that both managers and writers can agree are "project-oriented." *A Guide to the Project Management Body of Knowledge*, published by the Project Management Institute, offers an excellent definition of projects.

A project is a temporary endeavor undertaken to create a unique product or service [1].

Using this and other definitions [2], it is possible to isolate some important characteristics underlying projects. Most writers on project management point to four common characteristics:

- They are constrained by a finite budget and time frame; that is, they typically have a specific budget allocated and a defined start and finish date. Further, their budgets often represent a significant portion of the resources of the performing organization.
- They comprise a set of complex and interrelated activities performed by diverse resources or organizational members that require coordination.
- They are directed toward the attainment of a clearly defined objective or set of objectives which, when achieved, mark the end of the project and the dissolution of this project team.
- To some degree, each project is unique.

These features form the core that distinguishes project-based work from other forms of organizational activity. Because they are significant and underscore the inherent challenge in managing projects, it is important to examine each of these characteristics in more detail. In developing a general understanding of projects, the roots of conflict embedded in the characteristics of projects themselves will emerge.

## Finite Budget and Schedule Constraints

Unlike ongoing operations that occur within "line," or functional units of most corporations, projects are set up with two important bounds on their activities: a specified time period for completion and a limited budget. Projects are temporary undertakings, intended to solve a specific problem, not to supplant the regular functional operations of the organization, but rather to operate until the goal is to accomplished. Once these objectives have been achieved, the project ends.

Certainly, we should note that budget and time constraints are estimates, based on the best available—sometimes naively optimistic—information the organization has. As a result, it is not uncommon to build in a margin for error to allow for unforeseen expenses or time slippage.

Given the significant portion of an organization's budget that projects often comprise, it is clear that in making budget and project selection decisions there is a strong propensity for conflict. There are bound to be differences in opinion as to how scarce resources such as money and personnel are used. One obvious reason is that in making such choices we are implicitly, and many times explicitly, making trade-off decisions. It is impossible for the manager to give approval and funding to two competing projects. The decision is made on the basis of a number of criteria that will put the two potential projects, and their prospective project managers, into conflict.

## Complex and Interrelated Activities

Projects typically comprise a degree of complexity not found in other functional departments, often due to the cross-functional nature of the activities. For example, in developing a new product, a project team may be staffed by employees from a variety of functional backgrounds: marketing, production, finance, human resources, and others. This cross-disciplinary nature of most project-based work adds another order of magnitude to the usual levels of complexity found within an individual department.

Unfortunately, the complexity and interrelatedness of projects has some unwelcome side effects: power, political processes, and conflict. Political activities and power considerations abound within projects due to the unique properties they possess as well as the multiple goals and attitudes of different members of the project team. Not only are projects forced to compete with functional units for a share of scarce resources but even within the project team the almost ubiquitous nature of conflict is clearly demonstrated. The project team regularly experiences these sources of tension and must seek a balance between dual allegiance to their functional boss and to the project manager.

Another example of the complex and interrelated nature of projects derives from the multiple activities that are carried out, often simultaneously, by different members of the project team. This interrelatedness is typified by the project network diagram used in the Critical Path Method, which demonstrates the sometimes bewildering array of interdependent activities performed by a project team. If tasks are not performed in the correct order and within the time allotted to them, the entire project can be jeopardized. Consequently, the project manager's job here is twofold: first, to establish a coherent working relationship among a number of team members from diverse functional backgrounds; second, to create a planning, scheduling, and control system that permits the greatest level of efficiency of project activities.

## Clearly Defined Objectives

Projects are usually created with a specific purpose or a narrowly defined set of purposes in mind. Indeed, the worst sorts of projects are those that are established with vaguely defined or fuzzy mandates that permit a wide range of interpretations among members of the project team and parent organization. Projects of this sort are usually doomed to spin along out of control as objectives are continually interpreted and reassessed while the budget grows and the estimated completion date slips further and further into the future.

An important bit of advice to organizations setting up project teams is to narrow their focus: make the objectives clear and concise. Indeed, it is usually better to create two project teams, each with a smaller set of clearly defined objectives, than to load excessively vague or expansive objectives on a single project. The more well-defined the objectives, the clearer are the indications, both internally and externally, that the project team is succeeding. We often find one of the features of projects that continue to "function" well past the point of serving any reasonable purpose is that either the initial objectives have been altered mid-stream or the objectives were so poorly stated when the project began, they provided no guidance for the team.

## Uniqueness

Projects are usually "one shot" propositions; that is, they are non-recurring and typically established to address a particular problem or market opportunity. Their uniqueness is the characteristic that underscores the challenge of project management—the learning curve from one project to the next is, at best, tenuous. Once a manager becomes part of a functional department involved, for example, with the production of Brand X, that manager will likely continue to face a series of duties and even problems that can be somewhat anticipated due to past experience with similar products manufactured using similar techniques. Past experience—either their own or others—and learning curves will allow that manager to begin to anticipate likely problem areas and points of potential difficulty in the production process. We are able to gain a measure of comfort with the company's manufacturing activities due to our familiarity with how the process has always operated.

The world of project managers is very different. Because we are faced with a unique problem or task, the "rules" for how the project should be run have not been developed. In effect, we have to learn some lessons as we progress. In learning these lessons and exploring virgin territory, project managers encounter the sort of risks and uncertainty that typify project-based work. It is, however, important to note that a project's "uniqueness" may vary considerably from company to company and project to project. A project team for a computer software manufacturer, for example, preparing the fourth upgrade and release of a well-known product will have the experiences of the original development team, plus the three modification teams to draw on in scheduling and coordinating activities. Certainly, recent demands for new features and advancing hardware technology have to be considered and represent a source of uniqueness, but the basic project shares common characteristics that limit the risk inherent in new product development.

## What is Project Management?

Given the nature and idiosyncrasies of projects as they have been explicated, how are we to define project management? Simply put, project management is the application of knowledge, skills, tools, and techniques to meet or exceed stakeholder requirements for the project [1]. This definition encompasses a number of distinct and often intimidating challenges. The successful management of projects is simultaneously a human and technical challenge, requiring a farsighted strategic outlook coupled with the flexibility to react to conflicts and trouble areas as they arise. Project managers who are ultimately successful at their profession must learn to deal with and anticipate the constraints on their project team and personal freedom of action while consistently keeping their eyes on the ultimate goal.

But what is the ultimate objective for project managers? What are the determinants of a successful project and how do they differ from projects we consider to be failures. Our initial definition of projects offers some important clues as to how we should evaluate project team performance. Any seasoned project manager will usually tell you that a successful project is one that has come *in on time, under budget, and performs as expected (conforms to specifications)*, commonly referred to as the triple constraint of project management.

In the last few years, we have seen a reassessment of this traditional model for project success. The old triple constraint is rapidly being replaced by a new model, invoking a fourth hurdle for project success: client satisfaction. Client satisfaction is the idea that a project is only as successful as it satisfies the needs of its intended user. As a result, client satisfaction places a new and important constraint on project managers who heretofore have often been evaluated through "internal" measures of success: budget, schedule, and performance. With the inclusion of client satisfaction as a fourth constraint, project managers must now devote additional time and attention to maintaining close ties with and satisfying the demands of external clients. Figure 1.1 illustrates the inclusive nature of project success through adding the fourth success measure.

An implication of this new "quadruple" constraint is its effect on traditional project management roles. Concern for the client, while important, necessitates that project managers adopt an outward focus to their efforts. In effect, they must not only be managers of project activities but now also sales representatives for the company to the client base. The product they have to sell is their project. Therefore, if they are to facilitate acceptance of the project and hence, its success, they have to learn how to engage in these marketing duties effectively.

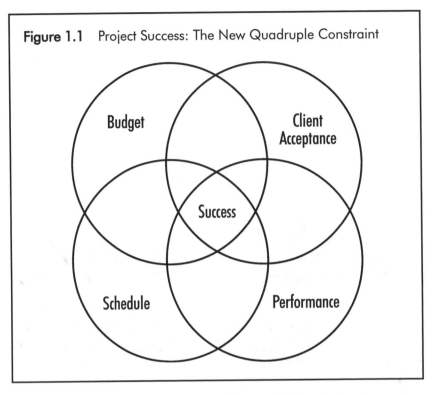

**Figure 1.1**  Project Success: The New Quadruple Constraint

When project management is viewed as a technique for implementing overall corporate strategy, it is clear that the importance of project management and project managers [3]. Project management becomes a framework for monitoring corporate progress as it further provides a basis on which the skillful manager can control the implementation process. No wonder, then, that there is a growing interest in the project manager's role within the corporation.

## The Project Life Cycle

The project life cycle is a common means of helping managers conceptualize the work and budgetary requirements of a project. The concept of life cycles is familiar to most of us; product life cycles— used to explain the sales life and demand for new products, organizational life cycles—used to predict the rise and demise of corporations, and so forth. Likewise, most projects pass through a

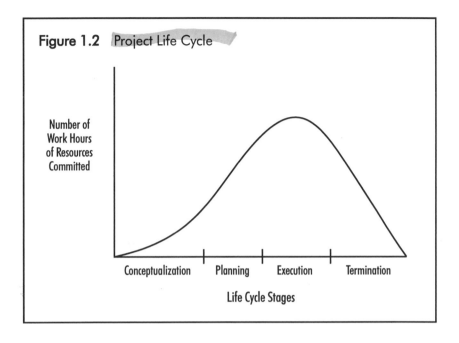

**Figure 1.2** Project Life Cycle

Number of Work Hours of Resources Committed

Conceptualization  Planning  Execution  Termination

Life Cycle Stages

similar life cycle that project managers find extremely useful for predicting resource needs and budget considerations.

Figure 1.2 is a representation of a project life cycle based on the four-stage model suggested by Adams and Barndt [4] and King and Cleland [5]. In their model, the project life cycle has been divided into four distinct stages or phases:

**Conceptualization.** This is the initial project stage. During a project's conceptualization, the initial objectives of the project are set as well as possible means to achieve these objectives. Project managers begin to make some personnel selections as they seek to staff their project teams. During the conceptualization phase of the project, actual resource outlay is low, as preliminary assessments are conducted. However, decisions made in this phase often have major impacts on the resources required in later phases and in the operation of the product of the project.

**Planning.** During the planning stage the project manager is busy conducting preliminary capability studies, assessing the objectives of the project in relation to resource and time constraints. As part of this

21

process, project managers will develop initial schedules, work breakdowns, assign specific tasks to team members. Further, they will make clear to the team how the concurrent and consecutive tasks are structured so team members are able to understand how their individual parts fit into the overall project development picture. Note in Figure 1.2 how the commitment of resources has begun to "ramp up" as increasing levels of money and other resources are committed to the project.

**Execution.** The third stage involves performing the bulk of the work of the project. Materials, people, and other necessary resources are procured and brought on line as they are needed. The various subroutines and other assigned tasks are being carried out in the proper sequence and performance capabilities of the product of this project are verified. During the execution stage, the project team is operating at maximum strength, with full resources brought into play. It is during this stage that the majority of the budget is spent and the physical product of the project is developed.

**Termination.** This is the final stage of a project. While the name suggests the project is finished, in reality, it is during a project's termination that a number of important tasks are performed. One of the most significant is the transfer of the project to its ultimate user— the client. Hopefully, as part of the project development process, the project team has kept the client closely informed of the performance characteristics of the product of the project and addressed any of their concerns to facilitate the transfer process. Also during the termination stage, the project manager begins releasing project resources back to the parent organization and reassigns project team personnel to other duties.

## How Are Project Teams Structured and Staffed?

One of the most intriguing and challenging aspects of project management is the relationship of the project team to the rest of the parent organization. With the exception of companies that have matrix or project structures, the majority of organizations using project management techniques employ some form of a standard functional

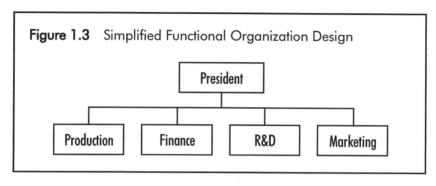

**Figure 1.3** Simplified Functional Organization Design

structure. As Figure 1.3 shows, within the classic functional structure, departments are organized in accordance with roles: marketing, finance, R&D, production, and so forth. Most activities and operations occur within these functional groupings. Further, these functional duties are often ongoing and act as necessary parts of the organization's activities. For example, the manager of new business development within the marketing department of a firm doing business with the federal government would be concerned with determining what programs the company will bid, what price it can offer, and the sort of product attributes it can reasonably deliver as part of those bids. In essence, no matter what program the company is bidding on, this activity becomes the manager's full-time job.

When project teams are added to an organization, structural rules change dramatically. Figure 1.4 demonstrates the same simplified functional structure in which project teams have been overlaid. Note the inclusion of the dotted lines from the functional departments of finance, R&D, marketing, and production. The implication of these lines is that when project teams are formed in most organizations that possess functional structures, they are staffed on an ad hoc basis from members of the various departments.

Personnel are assigned to project teams through one of several ways: their services are expressly requested by a project manager who values their competence, they are "exiled" to the project team by a functional boss who is dissatisfied with their work, or they are assigned because they are available. The key, however, is these assignments, like the projects themselves, are temporary. Personnel who staff the vast majority of project teams serve on those teams while maintaining links back to their functional departments. In fact,

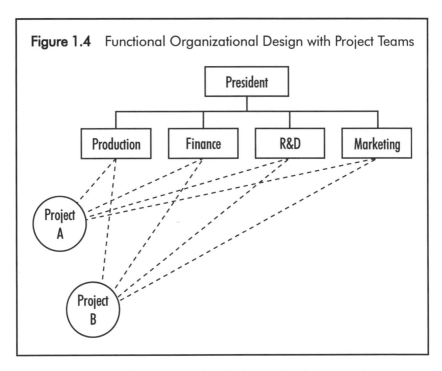

**Figure 1.4** Functional Organizational Design with Project Teams

it is quite common for these individuals to split their time between their project and functional duties. Not surprisingly, this arrangement can lead to a great deal of internal conflict within the project team as each person seeks to create a workable balance between the competing demands of direct supervisors and project team supervisors.

The temporary nature of projects, coupled with the very real limitations on the power and discretion most project managers have, constitutes the core challenge of managing projects effectively. Table 1.1 gives a comparative breakdown of some important distinctions between project-based work and more common department activities.

It is clear the issues that characterize projects as distinct from department work also illustrate the added complexity and difficulties they create for project managers. For example, within a department, it is common to find people with a more homogenous background; that is, the finance department is staffed with finance people, the marketing department is made up of marketers, and so on. On the other hand, most projects are staffed with special, cross-functional teams. These teams are composed of representatives from all the

**Table 1.1** Differences Between Department and Project Management

| Department | Project |
| --- | --- |
| Repeat process or product | New process or product |
| Several objectives | One objective |
| Ongoing | One shot—limited life |
| Homogenous | More heterogenous |
| Well established systems in place to integrate efforts | Systems must be created to integrate efforts |
| Higher certainty of performance, cost, schedule | Higher uncertainty of performance, cost, schedule |
| Part of line organization | Outside of line organization |
| Bastions of established practice | Violates established practice |
| Supports status quo | Upsets status quo |

Source: Graham, R.J. 1989. *Project Management as if People Mattered.* Bala Cynwyd, PA.: Primavera Systems, Inc.

relevant departments and each brings his or her own attitudes, time frames, learning, past experiences, and biases to the team. Creating a cohesive and potent team out of this level of heterogeneity presents a challenge for even the most seasoned and skilled project managers.

Likewise, functional activities are intended to reinforce the organizational status quo, the standard operating procedures that are clearly documented in most companies. Project management work is different. As Figure 1.4 shows, project teams operate at the periphery of the organization, pulling human, technical, and monetary resources away from the functional areas for their own needs. Rarely are manuals written on how these project teams are expected to operate. Rather, much of project management involves "violating" such sacred rules as the manner in which members of different functional departments are expected to communicate, the way additional resources are secured, interaction with clients by all members of the project team, and so forth. It is in violating these standard operating procedures that project teams are most effective, operating in a flexible and responsive manner to a variety of internal and external client demands.

As one continues to explore the nature of project management, it becomes increasingly clear that power and politics play a central role in the successful functioning of project managers. The balance of this book will lay out ways to understand and deal with politics, including its use in some of project management's most important activities: conflict resolution and negotiation.

## chapter 2

# Stakeholder Analysis and Project Management

**N**o manager makes decisions exclusive of consideration of how those decisions will affect external groups [1]. One way to understand the relationship of project managers and their projects vis-à-vis the rest of the organization is through employing stakeholder analysis. As a method for developing political acumen, stakeholder analysis is a useful tool for demonstrating some of the seemingly unresolvable conflicts that occur through the planned creation and introduction of any new project.

A project's stakeholders are "individuals or organizations that are involved in or may be affected by project activities" [2]. Consequently, when a company makes strategic decisions; it often will have major implications for a number of stakeholder groups; environmental watchdog groups, stockholders, government regulatory bodies, and others. Stakeholders can impact on and are impacted by organizational actions to varying degrees [3]. In some cases, a corporation must take serious heed of the potential influence wielded by some stakeholder groups. In other situations, a stakeholder group may have relatively little power to influence a company's activities.

The process of stakeholder analysis is helpful to the degree that it compels firms to acknowledge the potentially wide-ranging effects its actions can have, both intended and unintended, on various stakeholder groups [4]. For example, the strategic decision to close an unproductive manufacturing facility may make good "business" sense in terms of cost versus benefits. However, the decision to close the plant has the potential to unleash a torrent of stakeholder complaints

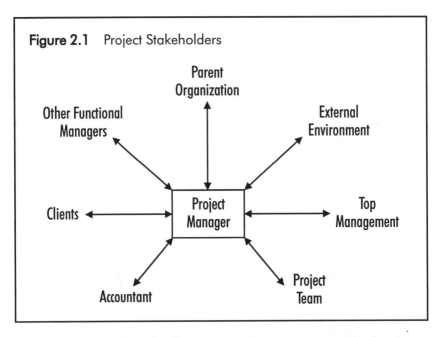

**Figure 2.1**   Project Stakeholders

including protests from local unions, workers, community leaders in the town affected by the closing, political and legal challenges, environmental concerns, and so forth. The prudent company will often consider the impact of stakeholder reaction as it weighs the sum total of likely effects from strategic decision.

Just as stakeholder analysis is instructive for understanding the impact of major strategic decisions, we can also use stakeholder analysis for our discussion of project management. When discussing the role of politics within the project environment, there is also real concern for the impact various project stakeholders can have on the project development process. This relationship is essentially reciprocal in that the project team's activities can also impact the external stakeholder groups [5]. For example, the project's clients, as a group, once committed to a new project's development, have an active stake in that project being completed on time and living up to its performance capability claims.

The client stakeholder group can impact project team operations in a number of ways, the most common of which are agitating for faster development, working closely with the team to ease project start-up problems, and influencing top management in the parent organization to continue supporting the project. The project team, in turn, can reciprocate this support by closely cooperating with the client and easing the transfer of the project to its intended user groups.

As illustrated in Figure 2.1, the key point for project managers is that, in addition to considering all the managerial activities involved in project development, they need to be aware of the ways in which attaining the project's goals can impact a host of external stakeholders outside their authority. Further, project managers must develop an appreciation for ways in which these stakeholder groups, some of which have considerable power and influence, can affect the viability of their projects. For example, there is an old saying in project management, "Never get the accountant mad." The obvious logic behind this dictum is that accountants can make the project manager's life easy or difficult, depending upon how closely they choose to monitor and control project expenditures.

This chapter explores the concept of stakeholder analysis as it forms a backdrop for project political behavior. Stakeholders, while having varying levels of power and influence over the project, nevertheless have the potential to exert a number of significant demands on project managers and their teams. This problem is compounded by the fact that the nature of these various demands quite often places them in direct conflict with each other.

In responding to the concerns of one stakeholder, project managers often unwittingly find themselves having offended or angered another stakeholder with an entirely different agenda and set of expectations. The challenge for project managers is to acquire the political skills to balance these various demands and to maintain supportive and constructive relationships with each important stakeholder group. Further, this chapter explores a strategy for identifying and specifically targeting each relevant stakeholder group.

## Identifying Project Stakeholders

In identifying project stakeholders, we must be as comprehensive as possible. Part of that process is looking beyond the project organization's internal environment to determine which external stakeholder groups can impact our operations and the degree to which they are able to influence the project's implementation.

Internal stakeholders are a vital component in any stakeholder analysis. Their impact is usually felt in positive ways; that is, while serving as limiting and controlling influences, most internal stakeholders want to see the project developed successfully. On the other hand, many external stakeholder groups operate in manners that are hostile to project development. Consider, for example, the case of a European city seeking to upgrade its subway system, adding new lines and improving facilities. There is strong potential for those interested in preserving antiquities to actively resist completion of the project if they perceive that tunnel digging could destroy valuable artifacts. Cleland [6] refers to these types of external stakeholders as "intervenor" groups and demonstrates that they have the potential to pose a major threat to the successful completion of projects.

Among the set of project stakeholders that project managers must consider are:

### Internal
- Top management
- Accountant
- Other functional managers
- Project team members.

### External
- Clients
- Competitors
- Suppliers
- Environmental, political, consumer, and other intervenor groups.

Consider the demands that these stakeholder groups commonly place on project managers. "Top management," as a single entity, is probably too simplistic a classification for this stakeholder group. Within top management there are differing degrees of enthusiasm for and commitment to the development of a particular project. Likewise, environmental intervenor groups are likely to be composed of a number of different factions, with their own agendas and priorities. In other words, a good deal of conflict and differences of opinion will be discovered within any generalized group. Nevertheless, this approach is useful because it demonstrates the inherent nature of conflict and other pressures arising from project development as it exists between stakeholder groups, and within groups.

**Top management.** The top management group in most organizations holds tremendous control over project managers and is in the position to regulate their freedom of action. Top management authorizes the development of the project from giving the initial "go" decision, sanctioning additional resource transfers as needed by the project team, to supporting and protecting the project managers and their teams from other organizational pressures. The top management group has, as some of its key concerns, the requirement that the project be timely (the project needs to be out-the-door on schedule), cost efficient, and be completed with minimal disruption to the rest of the organization.

In the case of significant projects, likely to consume a large portion of an organization's capital budget, there is a strong potential for top management to be split in their support. Project managers have to find ways to not only placate the concerns of top management but, more important, to isolate members of the top management group who have the greatest potential impact on the ongoing viability of the project.

Who are the project's advocates?

Who are its opponents?

Is there a strategy to control the detrimental effects that top management opponents may have on my ability to successfully conclude the project?

Is there support of friendly members of the top management team to serve as champions or advocates?

These are some important questions canny project managers must consider at the advent of a project in evaluating relations with the top management team.

**Accountant.** The accountant's raison d'être is maintaining cost efficiency from the project team. Accountants support and actively monitor project budgets and, as such, are often perceived as the enemy by project managers. This perception, while common, is wrong-minded. Accountants perform an important administrative service for the project manager and team in tracking costs and expenditures. Savvy project managers should work to make an ally of accountants rather than assume that they serve in adversarial capacities.

**Functional managers.** The functional managers who occupy line positions in the traditional chain of command represent an important stakeholder group that project managers must recognize. Most projects are staffed by individuals who are essentially on loan from their departments. In many cases, project team members are only part-time appointments to the team, because their functional managers expect 20-hours per week in performing their functional responsibilities. This situation can create confusion and seriously divide loyalties among team members, particularly if their performance evaluation is conducted by the functional manager rather than the project manager. For survival, team members are likely to maintain closer allegiance to their functional group rather than to the project team.

Project managers need to appreciate the power of an organization's functional managers as a stakeholder group. Functional managers, like the accountants, are not usually out to actively torpedo project development. Rather, they have loyalty to their functional roles operating within the traditional organizational hierarchy.

**Project team members.** The project team obviously has a tremendous stake in the project's outcome. Although they may have a divided sense of loyalty between the project and their functional group, in many instances these team members volunteered to serve on the project and are receiving challenging work assignments and opportunities for growth that will motivate them to perform effectively.

Just as top management and the accountants have their priorities, the project team's concerns focus on the need to get the project "right." Hence, they desire as much time as the project manager can secure for them. Top management seeks deadlines—project teams prefer to avoid them. Further, the project team wants the client to "lock in" to project specifications as early as possible. It is much easier for project team members to operate if they are reasonably sure the client will not be changing specs nor asking for new features or additions to the project after it begins.

**Clients.** Clients are concerned with receiving the product of the project as quickly as possible. And if costs are not passed on to them, they are not overly interested in the expense of the project's development. On the other hand, they want to make suggestions and request alterations in the project's features and operating characteristics for as long as the project manager and team are willing to listen. Clients feel, with justification, that a project is only as good as it is acceptable and is usable by them. As a result, they demand flexibility and willingness from the project team to be amenable to specification changes.

**Competitors.** Competitors can be an important stakeholder if they are materially affected by the successful implementation of a new product. Should a rival company, for example, bring a new product to market first, the project team's parent organization could be forced to alter, delay, or even abandon its project.

In assessing competitors as a project stakeholder group, project managers seek to uncover what information is available concerning the status of potential rival projects being developed within competing firms. Further, the lessons learned by competitors can be an important, useful source of information for a project manager who is initiating a similar project in another company. If a number of severe implementation problems or cost overruns occurred during the first organization's project, that information could offer valuable insight to the other project organization in terms of what activities or steps to avoid in its own situation.

**Suppliers.** "Suppliers" is any group providing raw materials or other resources the project team needs to complete their project. If the project requires a significant supply of externally purchased components, it is important for the project manager to take every step possible to ensure steady deliveries. In large-scale construction projects, for example, project managers must face and satisfy an enormous number of supplier demands. Companies that routinely bring in materials for projects have to consider vendors as important stakeholders. Part of the project manager's job in this type of project is to make certain the project team will continue to have the raw material resources to continue project development.

**Intervenor groups.** Any environmental, political, social, community-activist, consumer group, and federal, state and local regulators that can have a positive or negative effect on a project's development and successful launch are "intervenor groups" [6]. That is, they have the capacity to intervene—including the judicial system—in a project's development and force their concerns to be included in the equation for project implementation. There are many examples of intervenor groups curtailing major construction projects, particularly nuclear power plant construction. Prudent project managers need to make an assessment of the nature of their projects and the likelihood that one intervenor group or another may make an effort to impose its will on the development process.

## Managing Stakeholders

The stakeholder management process consists of planning, organizing, directing, motivating, and controlling the resources necessary to deal with the various internal and external stakeholder groups. Figure 2.2 shows a model suggested by Cleland [6] illustrating the nature of the management process within the framework of stakeholder analysis and management. Cleland suggests these various stakeholder management functions are interlocked and repetitive— that is, this cycle is recurring. Identifying and adapting to stakeholder threats allows development of plans to better manage the challenges they pose. In the process of developing and implementing these plans new stakeholders, whose demands must also be considered, are likely to be uncovered. And, as the environment changes or the project enters a new stage of its life cycle, it may be necessary to cycle through the stakeholder management model again to verify that the original management strategies are still effective. If, on the other hand, the new circumstances make it necessary to alter those strategies, project managers must work through this stakeholder management model anew to update the relevant information.

## Developing a Political Management Strategy

In acknowledging the importance of stakeholder groups, project managers need to proactively manage the political nature of these groups' concerns. Block [7] offers a useful framework of the political process applicable to stakeholder management. Block suggests six steps prudent project managers should follow:
1. Assess the environment.
2. Identify the goals of the principal actors.
3. Assess your own capabilities.
4. Define the problem.
5. Develop solutions.
6. Test and refine the solutions.

34

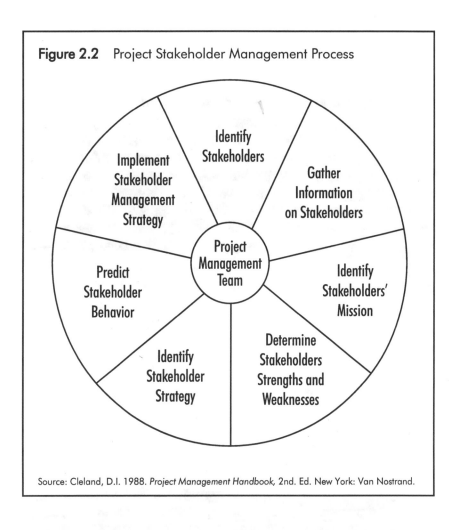

**Figure 2.2**   Project Stakeholder Management Process

Identify Stakeholders

Implement Stakeholder Management Strategy

Gather Information on Stakeholders

Project Management Team

Predict Stakeholder Behavior

Identify Stakeholders' Mission

Identify Stakeholder Strategy

Determine Stakeholders Strengths and Weaknesses

Source: Cleland, D.I. 1988. *Project Management Handbook,* 2nd. Ed. New York: Van Nostrand.

**Assess the environment.** This dictum implies that project managers must realistically determine the likely operating environment for administering the project. Is the project relatively low-key and not likely to attract attention or is it quite significant? A large computer manufacturer recently undertook to develop a new line of mainframe computers and storage units that could potentially lead to great profits or serious losses. In that environment, the manufacturer took great care to first determine the need for such a product line by conducting market research with corporate consumers. The result was a tremendous commercial success. Likewise, one of the reasons the Ford Taurus was so popular was Ford's willingness to create project teams that included consumers to more accurately assess their needs prior to project development.

From a political perspective, one important component of assessing the environment is to ask some central questions: Is this project politically sensitive, i.e., will it threaten the organization's status quo or the power balance of any important stakeholding group? and, What steps will begin to alleviate some of these groups concerns? Prudent project management demands an understanding that not all internal stakeholders equally perceive the project as important for the organization, nor do all the external stakeholders hold the same positive or, at worst, benign attitudes to the project's introduction.

**Identify the goals of the principle actors.** As a first step in fashioning a political strategy to defuse negative reaction, project managers should attempt to paint an accurate portrait of stakeholder concerns: a portrait that is predicated on honest assessment, not self-deception. Fisher and Ury [8] have noted that the positions various parties adopt is almost invariably based on need. What, then, are the needs of each significant stakeholder group regarding the project? Are their needs in line with those of the organization or are they more parochial, focusing on protecting turf or maintaining the status quo?

Project managers must also look for hidden agendas in goal assessment. Frame [9] has argued that all departments and stakeholder groups exert a set of overt goals that are relevant, but often illusionary. In their haste to satisfy these overt or espoused goals, a common mistake of untrained or novice project managers is accepting these goals on face value, without delving into the needs that drive them. In addition to probing the overt goals and concerns of various stakeholders, project managers must look for hidden agendas and other sources of constraint on implementation success.

Consider, for example, a project in a large, manufacturing company to develop a comprehensive project management scheduling system. The project manager in charge of the installation approached each department head and believed he had secured their willingness to participate in creating a centrally located scheduling system within the project management division. Problems developed quickly, however, because the MIS department staff, despite their public professions of support, began using every means possible to sabotage the implementation of the system. What was their concern? The belief that a computer-generated source of information anywhere outside their own department threatened their position as the sole disseminator of information.

**Assess your own capabilities.** What do we do well? What (if we are honest) are potential blind spots? Do we have the political savvy and a strong enough bargaining position to gain support from each of the stakeholder groups? If not, do we have connections to someone who can? Each of these questions is an example of the importance of understanding our own capacities and capabilities. Self-deception is one of the most pernicious causes of career destruction. And deceiving ourselves as to our capabilities, needs, or weak points, anything that can serve as a blind spot, can also lead to the failure of a project. Not everyone has the contacts to upper management that may be necessary for ensuring a steady flow of support and resources. If one honestly determines that political acumen is not a personal strength, the obvious solution is to find someone with that characteristic to help. Robert Burns once noted, "Oh wad some Power the giftie gie us/To see oursels as ithers see us!" Each of us needs to seek, as far as we are able, the power of the "giftie" in developing our political skills.

**Define the problem.** After assessing the overall environment, including the specifics of the principal players and our own capabilities, we can begin to fairly define existing, likely and potential problems. As is true in any project work, clearly defined goals are needed before beginning the task. If circumstances surrounding the project create uncertainties about the amount of labor a project will require, it's likely there will be problems between the accountant and the project team. Or when working in a delicate environmental area, conflict between outside intervenor groups, the client, and the project team is almost assured.

Theses sorts of issues and the role of each stakeholder need to be assessed before developing a strategy to manage their interest.

**Develop solutions.** There are two important points to note about this step. First, developing solutions means precisely that—creating an action plan to address the needs of the various stakeholder groups in relation to the other stakeholder groups. This is the stage where the project manager, together with the team, seeks to manage the political process. What will work in dealing with top management? In implementing that strategy, what reaction is likely from the accountant? The client? The project team? Asking these questions helps the project manager develop solutions that acknowledge the interrelationships of each of the relevant stakeholder groups.

Second, do the political homework first, prior to developing solutions. Note the point (stage five) when this step is introduced. Too often, project managers fall into the trap of attempting to manage a process with fragmentary or inadequate information. The philosophy of "Ready, Fire, Aim" seems to permeate many of our approaches to stakeholder management. The result of such an attitude is one of perpetual firefighting, during which the project manager operates like a pendulum, resolving one crisis after another. These project managers share one characteristic: they never reach a goal. The process of putting out one fire creates a new conflagration. Its "solution" sparks yet another blaze.

The bottom line in managing stakeholders is to create and maintain multiple strategies that provide project managers maximum flexibility. The more these strategies are refined and used as appropriate, rather than relying on one approach regardless of circumstances, the better the chances of creating and managing constructive relations with project stakeholders.

**Test and refine the solutions.** Testing solutions implies acknowledging that the project manager and team are operating with imperfect information. We assume stakeholders will react to certain initiatives in predictable ways. Obviously, such assumptions are often erroneous. In testing and refining solutions, the project manager and team must realize that solution implementation is an iterative process. We make our best guesses, test for stakeholder reactions, and reshape our strategies accordingly.

Many preconceived notions about the needs and biases of various stakeholder groups must be refined as well. In some cases, our assessments are accurate. At other times, our suppositions may have been dangerously naive or disingenuous. Nevertheless, this final step in the stakeholder management process forces the project manager to perform a critical self-assessment. It requires the flexibility to make accurate diagnoses and appropriate mid-course corrections.

These six steps are an important method for assessing the role stakeholders play in successful project implementation. Each allows project managers to approach "political stakeholder management" as they would any other problem, recognizing it as a multivariate problem as various stakeholders interact with the project and with each other. Solutions to political management, using this methodology, are richer, more comprehensive, and more accurate in assessing the project stakeholders' concerns and the project manager's capabilities.

## Stakeholder Conflict

In developing a stakeholder analysis and political management strategy the essential, conflict in project development and implementation becomes clear. For example, assume a project has been undertaken in a company to implement a new information system. There are four identifiable stakeholder groups: top management, the accountant, the clients, and the manager's own implementation team. Top management has given the initial go-ahead to acquire and install the system. Likewise, the accountant provides the cost control and support for the implementation effort, ensuring that budgets are maintained and project costs are near projected levels. The clients are obvious stakeholders as intended users of the new system. Assuming an implementation team is working to put the information system on-line, this team itself is a stakeholder in the implementation if they are being evaluated for their efforts.

The nature of the conflict among stakeholder groups is illustrated by focusing on three criteria by which the implementation project effort will be evaluated: schedule, budget performance, and system performance specifications. Schedule is the projected time to complete the installation and get the system on-line. Budget performance refers to the implementation team's adherence to initial projections for the information system implementation. System performance specification involves the assessment that the project is up and running, plus performing the range of tasks for which it was acquired. Certainly, additional evaluative criteria can and should be employed. These three success measures, however, demonstrate the nature of the underlying conflict in project implementation.

**Figure 2.3** Stakeholders' Conflicting Demands

| | Cost | Schedule | Performance |
|---|---|---|---|
| Top Management | ↓ | ↓ | — |
| Accountant | ↓ | — | — |
| Client | ↓ | ↓ | ↑ |
| Implementation Team | ↑ | ↑ | ↓ |

Legend: ↑ Significant stakeholder interest
↓ Limited stakeholder interest
— Neutral

Figure 2.3 shows the four identified stakeholders and the three success criteria that have been selected. The arrows show the emphasis placed on each of these criteria by the stakeholders. Consider the case of stakeholder preferences and the differences between clients and the implementation team. It is obvious that in terms of evaluation criteria such as schedule and budget there are significant differences in attitude—the clients want the system delivered as soon as possible at the lowest possible cost. On the other hand, the implementation team would like larger budgets and more time. The importance of performance specifications will vary with stakeholder group. Clients want the opportunity to alter the system, customize it, or add as many technical capabilities as possible. The implementation team is more comfortable with a simple system that has few technical surprises—less likely to have long debugging procedures—and is not changed once it has been acquired.

Figure 2.3 presents a compelling portrait of the underlying conflict of most project implementation efforts. It also illustrates one inescapable conclusion: To rationalize and resolve the diverse goals and priorities of various stakeholders, a considerable amount of bargaining and negotiation is called for. Bargaining and negotiation are two of the primary methods of resolving conflict in organizational politics. Clearly, political behavior is required for successful implementation efforts. A successful project manager is not one who will satisfy all stakeholder parties. Implementation success is instead predicated on the project manager's ability to successfully bargain and negotiate with various stakeholders to maintain a balance between their needs and the realities of the project.

Project implementation is a process that depends on the project manager's clever and effective exercise of political skills and recognizing, as Figure 2.3 shows, it is not possible to keep every stakeholder happy. When the client is happy with the number of specification changes the project manager is willing to make, the team is likely to be upset by the manager's unwillingness to freeze specifications. Likewise, when the team is satisfied with the amount of time the project manager has scheduled for the development process, the manager is likely to hear complaints from top management about lagging schedules. As a result, rather than seek general happiness from each stakeholder group, the true goal of project managers should be to keep everyone minimally annoyed! If everyone is minimally upset with the project manager's handling of various components of the project—time, budget, and specifications—it is likely an effective balance among the various competing demands has been found.

Another aspect of this balance is that not all stakeholders have equal priority. Figure 2.3 makes no distinctions about primacy of goals amongst groups. In reality, modern project management recognizes the client as the final determinant of project success and is (almost) always the most important stakeholder. Consequently, in balancing stakeholder requirements, project managers must consider the question of trade-offs among the various groups. It is possible, for example, to give the client additional specification changes, even at the risk of offending the accountant, if, in the project manager's opinion, such concessions will lead to a strong long-term relationship. In this instance, the project manager may be willing to anger the accountant in the interest of future work.

This "importance" should somehow be attached to each of the clients when making trade-off decisions. Our goal is to take these importance weights into account while seeking to minimize "weighted dissatisfaction" [10].

## Summary

The management of project stakeholders represents a political challenge most project managers are only now beginning to acknowledge. Part of the reason for this is that little is known about the nature of the various project stakeholders: who they are, what their separate agendas are, and how to understand the nature of project stakeholder trade-offs. This chapter presents a framework for understanding some of the best known project stakeholder groups, arguing that the stakeholder management process is cyclical, requiring that project managers continually update and reassess the nature of the stakeholder groups and their potential impact on the project. It also suggests a methodology for more comprehensive management of stakeholders as a political challenge, and offers a model illustrating the compelling nature of project stakeholder trade-offs. Different stakeholder groups have different priorities which project managers must acknowledge. Behind this is the tacit understanding that it is manifestly impossible to "maximize" satisfaction levels among all stakeholders. Insightful project managers must find a delicate balance of trade-offs, seeking to satisfy all groups only to the degree possible.

## chapter 3

# Power and the Project Manager

A n exercise often used in management training sessions on power is to begin by asking, "How many people here like power?" The class's typical response is interesting and instructive. One or two people immediately shoot their hands upward. The majority of the group shuffle about, look around at classmates, and finally raise their hands with a certain timidity, as if admitting that liking power is a fault to be confessed. Another small group resolutely refuses to raise their hands at all, often professing they simply do not like "controlling" or "manipulating" others.

This is one of the central problems with discussing power—few of us are entirely sure what power actually means. We understand its effects and occasionally are horrified by its blatant misuse, but we are uncertain of its actual characteristics. As a result, "power" lends itself to such misinterpretation and misunderstanding that it is difficult to discuss the subject objectively.

Power is the ability to get activities or objectives accomplished in an organization in the way one wants them done. Some definitions of power frame the term as a confrontational issue—the belief that power implies forcing someone to do something they would not ordinarily do. Another definition of power is more benign, stating that power is a mechanism to move an individual or company off dead-center. Underlying these definitions of power is the belief that power "enables" some members of an organization to pursue objectives. Whether those objectives are for the good of an organization or are purely self-centered is another issue. Nevertheless, as part of any discussion of the project management process, it is important to understand the nature of power in organizations, its various bases, how one gets and holds power, and its potential effects on power holders.

## Power vs. Influence

Influence and influencers are pervasive in our society. Television and radio advertisements, televangelists, and salespeople represent examples of some of the most common types of influence we experience daily. None of these influencers can *force* your compliance. Each of us has the power to change the channel or leave the store if we are offended or threatened by the influencer's message. Why, then, are many of these people so successful in raising money and gaining sales? In a different context, how can we explain the seemingly mystifying success some of our peers have in gaining compliance from other organizational members, often even without direct authority over them? The answer typically focuses on the greater ability to influence some of us possess relative to others.

Because influence is a key component of organizational life, it is important to distinguish between influence and power before considering the role of power in organizations. Many managers define power in terms of influence as a convenient shorthand. More appropriately, we can view influence as one's ability to get another to do something we want when there are no gross power differences between the two parties. That is, the influencer has no formal ability to "force" the other person to seek some goal or perform some task. From this definition, it is clear that there are some important similarities between power and influence—both are used to change another's behavior. The two constructs, however, are very different in some important ways. Each demonstrates that a thorough knowledge of influence tactics are important tools for better managing within the organization's political climate.

Table 3.1 demonstrates some of the relevant differences between power and influence. These differences are classified under three headings: scope and generality, strength of foundation, and tenure.

*Scope and generality* refer to the nature of how one uses influence versus power. Typically, successful influencers are situation-specific. That is, those who are adept at influencing others know intuitively when and under what circumstances to attempt to change someone

**44**

Table 3.1 Power versus Influence

| | Power | Influence |
|---|---|---|
| 1. Scope and generality | Cuts across situations and relationships | Situation specific and usually face-to-face |
| 2. Base of use | Strong base. Does not have to be done well to work | Weak base. Must be used well or will not work |
| 3. Tenure | Long-term | One shot deal |

else's behavior. Good influencers do not misuse or overuse their abilities because they know the more often they employ them, the more likely that co-workers will begin to refuse to comply with their wishes. Remember, the use of influence implies that one party does not have any formal authority to force a point of view on the other—compliance is purely voluntary.

In addition, good influencers rely almost exclusively on face-to-face meetings. There are two primary reasons for meeting rather than using telephones or other media. First, it is harder for the average person to refuse another during direct contact. Memos or telephone calls offer an impersonal approach, making it easier to refuse an influencer's requests. Second, good influencers are invariably adept at reading body language and other nonverbal responses from their "target." Good influencers in action are constantly altering the "angle of attack" or promotional pitch as they perceive that one line of argument is either likely to be accepted or rejected. This sensitivity to the other individual's reactions is not possible without direct contact.

Power does not accept the constraints of situation and approach. When one individual has power over another, that person is in a position to operate without regard to concerns about scope and generality. The "boss," or power holder, is in a position to force compliance regardless of the situation and via any means. For the power holders the telephone is just as effective as face-to-face meetings.

Another distinction between influence and power can be seen in *strength of foundation*. This concept refers to the fact that influence, in order to be effective, must be used well; that is, because one's base (or foundation) of actual power over another may be weak, effective planning, preparation, and role playing must be substituted to influence another.

Power, on the other hand, gives a manager a strong base from which to operate. The manager with power does not have to be constrained to exercising that power in clever or situation-specific ways. He or she tells another to do something and that subordinate is bound to comply. Further, because the power base is strong, power holders do not have to be particularly sensitive in using their authority. "Do it because I say so!" may be all the information the power holder is required to convey.

Another difference between power and influence is its *tenure*. Power is much longer lived than influence. Because influence is situation-specific, it is used sparingly. To overuse influence, particularly with any individual or group, is often to lose it. On the other hand, power lasts. Managers occupying higher positions in an organizational hierarchy have practical power over those in a lower echelon.

How can managers recognize influence tactics, particularly when those tactics are directed at them? Or, put another way, given these distinctions between power and influence, what are some of the more common forms of influence? There are several common approaches to influence, with three underlying characteristics; each works best in face-to-face settings, they are situation-specific, and they implicitly assume the influencer cannot directly force his or her will on the other person. Among these common approaches are:

**Persuasion**—simply arguing the merits of one's position with another. Persuasion suggests that if the one person will simply give a fair hearing to the influencer, he or she will be won over on the strength of the argument.

**Ingratiation**—the art of flattery, cajolery, or a search for common ground to win favor and gain another's willingness to cooperate. Ingratiation, as an influence tactic, offers the simple argument that it is easier to catch flies with honey than vinegar. For example, a project manager working for the Chrysler Corporation made a point of saving all personnel notices like transfers, promotions, and awards of advanced degrees. He filed them away and prior to calling on another manager or executive for the first time, always read up on relevant information concerning that person. Thus, he knew their educational background, where they were from, and something about their work history. This tactic gave the project manager a terrific source of common ground and talking points, making contacts cooperative and supportive of his needs.

Another interesting example of ingratiation as an influence tactic has been termed the Theory of Wooden Nickles [1]. One of the smartest moves for new employees is to do a favor for the boss' secretary, the custodian, and the manager in human resources who performs job studies. To illustrate, one bright young engineer once made a point of fixing a squeaky pencil sharpener that several other engineers had demanded the custodian repair, a job he had tried and failed at several times. That simple act of helping the custodian was reciprocated more than once as the custodian went out of his way to find ways to show his appreciation. Over the course of the next year, the young engineer received a private office and needed pieces of office furniture, all scouted out for him by the same custodian he had helped.

**Pressure**—a form of influence that applies external considerations as a supplement to the message itself; for example, time constraints. Pressure tactics frequently seek to limit the target's freedom of choice or movement in order to gain compliance. A salesman who claims a product will be on sale for a limited time is hoping the added pressure of the time constraint will reinforce the influential message.

**Guilt**—a powerful but sometimes overlooked form of influence, guilt implies a relationship based on obligation between two parties. As a result, one may attempt to sway the other by an appeal to this sense of duty or obligation, regardless of whether obligation actually exists.

## Sources of Power

An early, extremely influential study in organizational behavior sought to characterize the various "bases" of managerial power that one can potentially possess. Although slightly modified over the years, the basis of this study is still important to our understanding of exactly how managers can acquire power. French and Raven [2] point to two distinct bases of managerial power: personal and positional. Personal power, they argue, refers to the power that comes to an individual from a number of sources. This sort of power is manifested through a manager's relations with others in the organization.

Positional power, on the other hand, is the power accrued through formal organizational authority channels.

There are a number of different forms of personal power, which managers can acquire in varying degrees. Among the more well-known personal power bases are referent power, expert power, information power, and connection power.

Referent power refers to the situation where other organizational members like someone and want to be like them. The power-holder acts as a reference point for others. Referent power is a significant, often used, form of power. Advertisers use of star athletes to endorse products illustrates the fact that a large percentage of people in our society are swayed by the opinions of those they hold in high regard. Adolf Hitler's charismatic presence and oratorical abilities gained him a measure of personal power long before he became first chancellor and later dictator of Nazi Germany. And within organizational circles, examples of referent power can be found at all levels of the organization. When members of a loading dock gang gravitate toward a friendly or physically large co-worker, we find evidence of referent power. When a junior manager willfully confronts a superior and is lionized by co-workers for having the guts to stand up to the boss, he is experiencing a level of referent power. In all of these examples, the power-holder is one who has the ability to sway the opinions of others through the dynamism of personal power—power that is evidenced by the regard with which the power-holder is held by other members of the organization.

A second form of personal power is expert power. This is the belief that the power-holder has some expertise or knowledge that others need to perform their jobs. An example of expert power can be found within the R&D departments of many organizations. Individuals who are generally regarded by their peers as having expert knowledge will typically wield far more *real* power in the laboratory than the designated lab manager, particularly if the designated manager is not perceived to have as great a level of expertise.

Informational power is another form of personal power, similar to expert power. It is defined as the belief that the power-holder either possesses or has access to information necessary to perform a job. Some managers serve as the conduit for all forms of organizational information. Whether that information is conveyed in memos, gossip and hallway rumors, or direct access to upper management, these individuals hold power because they possess this information. Other organizational members are willing to defer to them to the degree that they perceive that this information, whether gossip or activity-based, is relevant and useful for their own work and organizational survival.

The final type of personal power is known as connection power. The power of connections is clear in all organizational settings. Some individuals, regardless of their formal position, possess tremendous power due solely to their connections to powerful people. The classic adage, "It isn't *what* you know, it's *who* you know," succinctly states the importance of connections as a source of power with peers and superiors.

Each of the personal power bases have a common feature—the "power" found in each derives directly from human relationships. By definition, unless one willingly explores relationships with peers and superiors in organizations, one cannot reasonably expect to develop any form of personal power.

These personal power bases offer project managers a wide range of options. Not everyone is blessed with a magnetic personality making it easy to cultivate and maintain referent power. Likewise, some people are adept at creating a network of powerful connections while others, either through personality or external circumstances, do not have similar opportunities. On the other hand, acquiring information or developing expertise is within the control of most managers and should be explored as alternative bases of power.

Positional power, as opposed to personal power bases, is specifically derived from the position a manager holds within the organizational hierarchy. As a result, we often think of positional power as a manager's more "formal" base of power. Included in positional power are the bases of legitimate power, reward power, and coercive power. Legitimate power is the hierarchical authority managers can "legitimately" expect to wield as a perquisite of positions they occupy in the chain of command. Reward and coercive power are the natural manifestations of the legitimate authority that one who occupies a position with organizational power should naturally have as part of that power—the dual rights of reward and punishment.

Within the arena of project management the whole issue of positional power becomes problematic. Project managers in many organizations operate outside the standard functional hierarchy. While that position allows them a certain freedom of action without direct oversight, it has some important concomitant disadvantages, particularly as it pertains to positional power. First, because cross-functional relationships between the project manager and other functional departments are ill-defined, project managers often quickly discover they have little or no legitimate power to simply force their decisions through the organizational system. Functional departments usually do not have to recognize the legitimate right of project managers to interfere with functional responsibilities. In these cases project managers hoping to rely on positional power to implement their projects are quickly derailed.

Secondly, in many organizations, project managers have minimal authority to reward their team members who, because they are temporary subordinates, maintain direct ties and loyalties to their functional departments. In fact, it is depressingly commonplace for project managers to not even have the opportunity to complete a performance evaluation on temporary team members. Clearly, in such an environment, project managers' promises to subordinates of rewards for outstanding performance are at best tentative. Likewise, project managers may have minimal authority to punish inappropriate behavior. They discover, in short order, that they have neither the ability to offer the carrot nor threaten the stick. The implications here are clear: project managers hoping to effectively lead a temporary project team composed of cross-functional subordinates are almost always forced to develop strong influence skills and cultivate personal power bases as a tactic for enhancing their status and credibility.

## Other Sources of Power

In addition to the sources of power French and Raven identified, more recent research has pointed to additional sources for developing power in an organization. These different power tactics offer project managers several specific ways to enhance their power.

One important method for acquiring additional power is through centrality. Centrality refers to the knowledge that those who occupy central, or visible, positions within an organization naturally acquire a

50

degree of power over other less visible members. Canny managers seek to locate themselves centrally in an organization and surround themselves with a network of allies and loyal subordinates. For example, clearly a manager will develop more power through being assigned to a job at corporate headquarters rather than a small satellite office. The more central the position, the more others must go through that person to achieve their own needs; hence, the more power that individual will wield. Managers must walk through the avenues of power if they are ever to accrue their own power.

Another method for gaining power is by maintaining a reputation for *nonsubstitutability.* That is, the belief—whether true or erroneous—of other key organizational members that the manager occupies some position or performs a task that is indispensable. If other managers depend upon some individual for their own resources or other services, that person will have a greater degree of authority. A classic example of this point is found within many organizations that have a substantial computer operation or use a large-scale MIS system. Those involved in these organizations quickly discover that certain computer experts seem to have power far beyond their position simply because they are the only people who can make the computer work, generate needed information, or provide vital logistical support services.

## The Effects of Power: The Good, The Bad, and The Ugly

Pursuing and maintaining power is not always a positive experience, nor does everyone who has power use it wisely or for the greater good of the organization. In assessing the effects that acquiring and using power can have on managers, one business writer [3] used the framework from a well-known western movie, *The Good, The Bad, and The Ugly*. In the movie, three rather ruthless men compete with each other for a fortune in gold. In corporate life, managers often compete with each other for power. Unfortunately, as we allow ourselves to become caught up in this pursuit, we may not be aware of the effects of power on our own lives.

## The Good

Quickly, what is good about power? When most managers consider that question, they usually conclude that power gets things done. Power is the engine that drives the organizational machinery. Without it there is little or no incentive to make necessary changes, initiate projects, or push the organization into uncharted but potentially lucrative waters. Power gives managers the ability to move the machine forward, and it is a vital component of any manager's repertoire. As McClelland noted in his research, successful managers have a greater need for power than for affiliation; that is, they understand that it is more important to maintain control than it is to be personally liked.

## The Bad

One of the negative consequences of wielding power is its effect on us, both as managers and human beings. Slevin [3] noted, "Power has its price." The quest for power in organizations is emotionally and physically draining; one writer noted that the drive for success is one of the greatest sources of anxiety in our society [4]. Why does power do this to us? The quest for power is, by definition, fraught with conflict. One cannot gain power without gaining advantage, usually at another's expense. Over time, this quest has severe implications for our mental and physical health. The "good news" evidence of our stress will appear in very noticeable ways. For example, changes in behaviors, physical side effects (ulcers, hypertension, high blood pressure), and psychological effects (depression, aggression, etc.) all serve as powerful signals that somewhere we have gone off the track. Our body and mental apparatus operate as a "circuit breaker" mechanism to signal we may be experiencing some of the bad effects of power.

## The Ugly

The ugly side of power offers a potentially frightening message—power changes us. It leads to noticeable and real changes in our attitudes about ourselves and others. Most of us have heard Lord Acton's famous aphorism, "All power tends to corrupt and absolute power corrupts absolutely." This insight is not new, the ancient Greeks had a term for the effect that power has on creating an overweening pride and self-absorption—hubris. Sophocles' play *Oedipus Rex* demonstrates the effect that ugly power can have on ordinary and even heroic individuals.

For many people acquiring power is intoxicating, they begin to experience an altered mind-state in which they see themselves as superior to others. At the same time, while craving the approval of subordinates and other less powerful individuals, they also begin to denigrate these people because they do not have the same level of power. The ugly side of power gives us an exalted view of ourselves and transmits feelings of contempt for those we deem "less worthy."

Slevin has noted four specific ways in which power can corrupt:

1. **People acquire a "taste for power" and relentlessly pursue more power as an end in itself.** In the movie *Wall Street*, the character played by Charlie Sheen, Bud Fox, had a climactic meeting with Gordon Gecko, the insidious and manipulative financier played by Michael Douglas. At a pivotal moment, Fox asked, "How much is enough, Gordon? How many yachts can you water-ski behind?" Clearly, there was no reason for Gecko to continue pursuing his predatory ways except that it was a style he had always employed. "Ugly" power-holders often have the same outlook. Power, itself, becomes the goal, not the means to another objective. In the process, the power-holders lose sight of the end for the process, amassing as much power as possible.

2. **Access to power tempts people to illegally use institutional resources as a means of enriching themselves.** Power-holders cannot discern between their own success and that of the organization they represent. Ultimately, they may not even care. The blurring of the lines between what is "mine" and what belongs to others is a very real problem because it reflects the twisting of "ugly" power-holders' priorities. Jim Bakker was a highly respected television evangelist who had built the PTL Club into a major, multimillion-dollar organization. Along the way, he forgot his role in the organization and began to treat the PTL Club as his own private source of funds and other perquisites. Bakker's fall from grace, brought on by the warping of his perceptions, is perhaps best summed up by a former associate who had known Bakker since his early days in the ministry. "Jim Bakker," he said, "is someone who started out loving people and using things and by the time of his arrest he was loving things and using people."

**3. People are provided with false feedback concerning their own worth and they develop new values designed to protect their power.** Those trapped in exercising the ugly side of power begin to surround themselves with a sycophantic crowd that continually reinforces the power-holder's self-delusionary perceptions. Bad news is conveniently forgotten or watered down so as not to interfere with this self-deception. Followers are generous with flattery and positive feedback and the power-holder may literally lose touch with the larger reality. In such a situation and surrounded by false feedback, it is hardly surprising the leader begins to conclude, "I am superior and more effective than those around me." Consider Manhattan hotel operator Leona Helmsley's remark, "Only the little people pay taxes," as an example of the sort of delusionary thinking that results from living in such a false reality. These thoughts often signal someone well on their way to the dangers of hubris.

**4. People with power devalue the worth of the less powerful and prefer to avoid close social contacts with them.** A fascinating side effect of ugly power is how it alters power-holders' opinions of others, especially those who are most constant in their flattery. One would suppose the power-holders would crave and value their followers' praise. Unfortunately, that conclusion is only half-correct. "Ugly" power-holders do, indeed, require an unending stream of praise and positive feedback, but at the same time they begin to devalue the feedback itself because it is offered by "inferiors." The contempt that "ugly" power-holders display for their followers in spite of, or perhaps *because of*, the unending litany of praise is another insidious side effect of ugly power. We need such praise but have nothing but contempt for the praise giver.

Ugly power is frightening in its corrupting potential. It is particularly frightening because, unlike the bad side of power which gives us physical and emotional signals of distress, ugly power, by definition, implies the power-holder has changed to such a degree that he or she becomes unaware they are caught in its throes. It creates managers with such egotism and self-inflated delusions that one would suppose the lessons would be clear for future managers. Unfortunately, that is not the case. It seems each generation of manager must learn their own lessons, sometimes the hard way. The good news is that those who are truly operating as "ugly" power-holders are a relatively small percentage of managers. The bad news is that for them, power has become an intoxicating end unto itself that is recreating them in an exceedingly unattractive form.

Power itself is neither good, bad, nor ugly. Power enables organizations and offers project managers opportunities to enhance their positions and their projects' chances of success. How power is used and its effects requires project managers to treat it with substantial respect, understanding what power can do *for* and do *to* those who wield it. Perhaps the first and most important analysis project managers need to make is an "internal check" to acknowledge their own needs and past experiences with power. As long as managers are willing to make an honest self-appraisal of their uses of power and reasons for acquiring it, they are likely to continue to use it in positive ways that work to their own and to the organization's advantage.

## Suggestions for Improving Your Power

What are project managers to conclude from the above discussion on power? Clearly, they can take away important insight for improving their own power base in what is often seen as a powerless job. Understanding the unique constraints faced by most project managers, there are some practical ways to begin expanding the power in the project management position.

### Make Yourself an Expert

One of the best, and often overlooked, methods for improving personal power lies in tapping into expertise. Although not everyone is charismatic and interpersonally acute and able to achieve referent power, practically every project manager *does* have the capacity to expand their power through the perceptions of others about their expertise. This power base can be readily acquired by those with the self-discipline to learn the technology of the project they are overseeing. Many project managers have failed in their assignments simply because their teams quickly realized that while they may have had a modicum of technical project skills, they did not understand the unique nature of the project well enough to give team members confidence in their decision-making abilities. Many project managers have lost all credibility with project team engineers because they could not speak to the technical problems associated with their projects.

Two contrasting examples best illustrate this point. In the 1980s two dynamic Silicon Valley firms were seeking to move from their original, entrepreneurial management styles into more professional and bureaucratic management practices. Both had been dominated by the vision and personality of their founders and had grown dramatically, to the point where the founders no longer had the time nor the inclination to manage the corporations on a day-to-day basis.

In seeking replacement CEOs, both companies went outside the computer industry, believing that a good manager can manage anywhere. In the first case, the organization was at the zenith of its power—appearing in 1981 as one of companies cited for "excellence" in Peters and Waterman's groundbreaking book, *In Search of Excellence*—when the founder stepped down. The new CEO, whose previous position was with a textile firm headquartered in New York City, came in and from the first day began stirring up the company. He demanded significant changes, many of which flew in the face of the original corporate culture and value set. Although he had no computer experience, he made several strategic moves that took the company away from its area of expertise and embroiled it in new battles on unfamiliar territory. Along the way, he succeeded in alienating his design staff and engineering departments, as they realized that despite all his public talk, he had no technical background nor any interest in learning how the technology worked. The organization entered a period of rapid decline, falling from industry leadership to filing for Chapter 11 bankruptcy protection in less than five years.

The second firm also went outside the industry in hiring its new leader. Although initially not an expert in the company's technology, the new CEO spent over six months learning the computer business and more importantly, learning computer technology, satisfying the engineering departments that they had a CEO who truly understood all aspects of the business. In acquiring expert power, this CEO was able to implement his ideas with a minimum of internal resistance, make significant strategic moves, and ultimately, lead the company into a new era of profitability.

What were the names of the two companies, one a lesson in failure and the other a continuing success story? Atari Corporation and Apple Computer. While it would be overly simplistic to suggest the only difference in these success and failure stories was the new CEO's willingness to become an expert, it also cannot be dismissed as purely coincidental. Expert power is important and can be acquired—and it must be maintained. There is nothing that will excite the contempt of technical team members faster than the perception that the project manager is either not an expert or is faking his expertise.

## Find Ways to Promote Your Project

Centrality is an important facet in acquiring power. Occupying a position central and visible to other corporate members can offer managers a nice "leg up" in establishing a base of power. The same principle holds true for a project. If a manager promotes his or her project as central to or important for organizational goals, that manager is in a better position to operate with a degree of power on their side, particularly in bargaining and negotiating with other department heads. One important caveat to this: In arguing for centrality, it is important to maintain personal credibility. It is a mistake for a manager to "over-hype" a relatively low-level project in the hopes of gaining just such a position of centrality. This is a classic example of the boy who cries "wolf" too many times. Other managers have a sense of the importance of various projects and to overuse the claim that a project is "critical" to the organization will eventually sacrifice a project manager's credibility. Use this approach sparingly.

## Don't Be Afraid to Promote Yourself

Every ambitious manager should find ways to become involved in activities with visibility. Personal reticence, the opposite of excessive self-promotion, serves managers no better in pursuing project goals. Some of us are loath to engage in personal advertising, believing that we should let our actions speak for themselves. This position is understandable, but usually wrong-minded. Managers have to come to an understanding of the difference between egotistically hyping achievements out of proportion and sitting stoically on the sidelines "waiting for the coach to put us into the big game." In promoting ourselves, there is nothing wrong with making clear to other, significant organizational members that we bring a solid track record to our projects and expect support and cooperation. The principle that applies here is that of nonsubstitutability—we are trying to demonstrate that as project managers we occupy our positions for good reason, are competent, and the right person for the job.

As a personal exercise, think of those considered to be "fast trackers," that is, those who seem to be moving rapidly up in corporate hierarchy. And realize one important criterion for fast tracking is the willingness to use self-promotion to an appropriate degree. Fast trackers want others, particularly top management, to know they are fast trackers. Their self-promotion is not simply the result of an ego run rampant, but an understanding that the more others perceive them as "up and coming," the more they will, in fact, move up the promotion ladder.

A young manager, for example, at a large auto manufacturing company became involved in that organization's Headquarters Management Club. Eventually, he volunteered to become Club Chairman. Although the duties contributed to his workload at corporate headquarters, the benefits he derived from the post, in terms of contacts made, were invaluable. He arranged for a company vice president to be a spotlight speaker at each meeting, leading to these influential people knowing his name and speaking with him on a first-name basis. Later, as a project manager, he had the unique ability when facing problems to gain immediate access to powerful individuals who could work on his behalf.

Project managers need to be willing to adopt a similar attitude of self-promotion, because such behavior serves the goals of their projects. As top management and functional managers perceive that the project manager is nonsubstitutable, they also begin to approach resource bargaining sessions on a more equal footing. While excessive "hyping" is liable to backfire as others begin to feel threatened, self-promotion done in moderation is an important source of organizational power. "Walking the walk" is crucial: "Talking the talk" makes subsequent actions easier.

## Enlist a Sponsor's Support

An important source of power derives from connections. Project managers should work to gain the support of a champion from within the organization hierarchy, preferably one who is significantly higher up the chain of command. Pinto and Slevin [5] discussed the importance of project champions as a key determinant of successful implementation. Both research and experience support this contention. In the majority of cases where a project was completed in a timely and relatively smooth fashion, it is possible to point to the support and active promotion of a senior manager.

A project sponsor needs to do more than send a memo to other functional departments, stating his or her support. True championing behavior consists of a willingness to intervene in development when necessary, contact other managers to enlist their cooperation, secure additional resources when crises occur, and serve as the head cheerleader for the project at high-level meetings. If such support is actively communicated, it can serve to ease many difficult situations in the implementation.

For example, one project manager and his mentor, the program director, had created a highly successful partnership. The project manager worked strenuously to "sell" a project to higher authorities. When they expressed a willingness to put the project on the books, his boss would visit each departmental vice president and ask what they were personally going to do to support the project. There was an underlying, veiled threat that unless the executive provided resources and political support, the program manager would not authorize the project to succeed. In this way, the two acquired both the financial resources and the political "pull" to ensure that their projects would be successfully implemented.

## Work to Establish Some Positional Authority

One of the favorite complaints of frustrated project managers is trying to operate with no formal authority. "No one will listen to me," "I have no pull with the functional managers," and, "Team members routinely put my requests on the back burner when their bosses snap their fingers," are all complaints stemming from the same source of frustration: lack of any formal, positional power. When considered in its proper context, it should never be surprising to project managers that they are often low person on the authority totem pole. And project team members often have two competing messages that are mutually exclusive: "I need you to work full-time on this project" versus "Forget the project. This week I need you full-time in the department." Every subordinate is going to make their choice based on self-preservation: Who has the power to reward and sanction me? In most organizations, that power rests exclusively with the department manager.

Rather than accept this limiting factor, project managers need to find ways to level the playing field between themselves and the team members' functional bosses. One method is to negotiate, as an early condition of taking on a project, the promise of being permitted to complete a performance evaluation on team members. While an obvious option, it is surprising how few organizations currently operate in this manner. Part of the reason for this is that functional managers actively resist surrendering any authority, fearing it will weaken their discretionary power. On the other hand, this is a chance for project managers to force upper management to actively back up their implied support for the project. Without the ability to offer rewards and punishments, even nominal ones in the form of a performance evaluation, project managers will never be in the position to operate with any real degree of status vis-à-vis their project team.

## Summary

Power is a complex, fascinating topic. Many of us are uncomfortable with it, fear it, or fear those who use it. This chapter has shown that power itself is simply a benign component of the organizational process. Bad past experiences with power or with those who had power over us tend to make us wary of employing power ourselves, oftentimes due to the belief that there is something unsavory about "controlling" the behavior of subordinates and project team members. Project managers need to develop a better understanding of the importance of a constructive attitude and learn how and how not to use power, then it can be better used, rationally and with minimal disruption to the organization. All projects depend on the responsible, effective use of power in order to be successfully concluded.

## chapter 4

# What is Organizational Politics?

ew topics generate as much heat and passionate feelings as a discussion of political behavior. Most organizational personnel are quick to condemn politics and their chief practitioners—company "politicians"—as predatory and counter to the interests of the organization. In fact, it is generally impossible to find individuals with even minimal organizational experience who have not had some bad experiences with office politics during their careers. In spite of most managers' familiarity and experiences with organizational politics, surprisingly little is known about the concept and its true impact on individuals within organizations.

One of the areas where politics is better understood—particularly its impact—is in the process of developing and implementing projects in organizations. A phenomenal amount of anecdotal and case study information exists that strongly reinforces the importance of understanding and effectively utilizing organizational politics as a tool in successful project implementation. Indeed, without an understanding of the role that power and politics plays in project management, the likelihood of managing the successful development of a project will be significantly diminished.

This chapter examines, in some detail, the bases of a project manager's personal power and the concept of organizational politics from the project management perspective, developing some of the more well-acknowledged themes that pervade the topic. No matter what definition of politics the reader uses, the end result is that political behavior is used as a method for dealing with basic organizational conflict. Unfortunately, while the practice of politics is often used to deal with conflict, the irony is that political behavior itself usually becomes a contributing cause of additional organizational conflict [1]. This chapter also presents a comprehensive overview of the power bases of project managers as well as a political framework for organizations, demonstrating the inherent nature of conflict in attempting to implement projects despite of a variety of project stakeholders. The chapter ends with suggestions to project managers on how to effectively operate within the political arena of organizations, not to achieve predatory and self-serving ends, but in an effort to smooth the process by which their systems are adopted.

## Power and the Project Manager

An additional discussion of power is warranted here because it is important to understand how power relates to the subsequent exercise of politics. When one examines the options that project managers are able to use in furthering their goals—the successful development of projects—it is both useful and instructive to consider their alternatives in terms of three modes of power: authority, status, and influence. This authority, status, and influence model was proposed by Robert Graham [2] as a way to make clear the methods by which project managers can achieve their desired ends. The model is valuable because it illustrates one of the key problems most project managers have in attempting to develop and implement their projects in corporations.

Authority is the type of power that accrues from the position occupied in the organization—positional power. In effect, if one individual sits higher on the organizational chart than another member of the project team, that person has some degree of positional power over the other. The nature of positional power, however, is extremely problematic within project management situations due to the temporary and "detached" nature of most projects vis-à-vis the rest of the formal organizational structure [3]. Project teams sit "outside" the normal vertical hierarchy, usually employing personnel on loan from functional departments. As a result, project managers have a much more tenuous degree of positional power within the organization. Other than nominal control over their own team, they do not have a corporate-wide base of positional power through which they can get resources, issue directives, or enforce their will. In most organizations authority as a power base cannot be relied upon with any degree of certainty.

Likewise, the second mode of power, status, is often problematic for project managers. Status implies the project manager, due to the nature, importance, or visibility of his or her project, can exert power and control over others in the corporate hierarchy as needed. And while some projects and project managers do, indeed, possess an enormous degree of status due to the importance of their projects (e.g., the project manager for the Boeing 777 program or the project manager for the recently completed Eurotunnel), the vast majority of project managers toil in relative obscurity, working to bring their projects to fruition while receiving little public recognition for their work. Most project managers cannot rely on status as a form of power and control over resources to enhance their project's likelihood of success. Despite obvious exceptions, the reality is very few projects or project managers can depend upon their status as a persuasive form of power.

The project manager's final form of control, influence, is an informal method for gaining compliance [4]. Project managers who use influence in furthering the goals of their project usually work behind the scenes, negotiating, cutting deals, or collecting and offering IOUs [5]. Influence, as a power tactic, is most readily used when managers have no formal positional authority to rely on. Hence, they are forced to use less formal means to achieve their desired ends. Influence is most widely seen as a power tactic in situations in which there is no obvious difference in authority levels among organizational members. To use an example from government, a president who is unsure of his degree of formal power and ability to force his legislative agenda through a recalcitrant Congress is likely to spend a great deal of time making back room deals and negotiating compromises. Dictators have no need to resort to using influence.

What is the implication of the authority, status, and influence model? Graham notes that the nature of project management work, the manner in which project managers and their teams are selected, and the relationship of projects to the formal organizational hierarchy force project managers to rely to a great degree on their ability to cultivate and effectively use influence as a negotiating and power tactic than either of the other two forms of power.

Formal, broad-based authority rarely exists for project managers to use in furthering their project's ends. Likewise, while some projects and/or project managers have the status to gain the resources they need, it is much less likely that the typical project manager, particularly younger members of the organization, will have enough status to affect any sort of change they desire. On the other hand, any project manager can learn to develop the skills to use influence as a power tactic. The key is realizing that influence is a form of corporate political behavior that can be used for the benefit of the project and, ultimately, the organization. To better understand the relationship between the use of informal influence tactics and political behavior, a comprehension of exactly what organizational politics implies is needed.

## What is Organization Political Behavior?

Few topics stir up as many sharply voiced opinions and general disagreement as the notion of corporate politics. Writers and researchers usually find that they cannot even agree on a uniform definition of politics, let alone acknowledge the role of politics in organizational life. When one sifts through the material on power and politics, a number of definitions are suggested; each with a varying degree of usefulness. Among the definitions of politics that are currently extant, some important patterns can be discerned which help establish a framework for understanding the concept. For example, one colleague has referred to politics as self-interested behavior with guile. Another definition suggests politics "involves those activities taken within an organization to acquire, develop, and use power to get one's way" [6]. Henry Mintzberg, another well-known researcher in organization theory, suggests politics encompasses modern organizations, referring to "system(s) captured by conflict" [7]. Yet another definition of politics characterizes political behavior as inherently competitive and focused on satisfying self-interests [8]. These and other definitions of the "negative school" generally portray political behavior as essentially malevolent, conflict-laden, self-aggrandizing, and unhealthy. The attitude can be summed up by the following arguments, suggesting that politics is:

*Behavior designed to benefit an individual or group at the organization's expense.* This idea suggests that political behavior is entirely self-serving, predicated on getting ahead in spite of the possible side effects to the organization as a whole. For example, a manager who continually violates production safety codes in order to increase efficiency and speed of operations may, in the short term, reap the benefits of achieving higher production quotas. However, should workers be injured, due to relaxed safety standards, both the company and the manager could be liable for substantial legal action. The short-term benefits of these acts are usually outweighed by long-term ethical and legal difficulties.

*The displacement of legitimate power.* "Legitimate" power is defined as the power that accrues to an individual from his or her position within the organization [9]. For example, bosses who rely on the position they occupy as a basis for giving orders are making use of legitimate power. Politics has the capacity to displace legitimate power through machinations designed to circumvent the conventional authority structure of the organization. For example, consider a situation in which a three-person chain of command exists: Sue is at the top, Bob is her subordinate, and Allen is Bob's subordinate. Allen would be exercising a political approach if he habitually found ways to "end run" Bob's authority by going directly to Sue to mediate disagreements, solve problems, or offer advice. Allen could use any of a number of ways to cultivate Sue's help, such as joining the same civic organizations, church, or country club. In an effort to create a personal relationship with Sue, Allen is banking on this relationship as a bulwark against Bob being able to use his legitimate authority. Allen has attempted to displace this authority through political behavior.

*The use of means not sanctioned by the organization to attain sanctioned ends, or the use of sanctioned means to obtain unsanctioned ends.* This proposition has two elements. First, it suggests political behavior might actually be used in the interests of the organization. This behavior would, however, be widely perceived as unethical or immoral. Recently, the chairman and CEO of Bath

Iron Works, a major shipbuilding company with extensive defense department contracts, resigned in disgrace following disclosure he had illegally accepted and made use of photocopied U.S. Department of Defense documents of a sensitive and secret nature which gave his firm an unfair advantage in bidding for new contracts. Obviously, it was in the interests of his company to win those contracts—sanctioned ends. Equally obvious, he violated the law—using unsanctioned means—in gaining this competitive advantage and, following his resignation, his company was forced to pay a substantial fine for his actions.

The second aspect of this proposition suggests that political behavior may involve the use of acceptable means to obtain unacceptable ends. Again, the issue here has to do with the degree to which political actors are willing to "bend" moral or ethical codes in order to gain an advantage. There are many actions an individual or organization can engage in that are legal but may be highly questionable from an ethical perspective. For instance, Johns-Manville Corporation received a great deal of bad press some years ago when, following the ban on the use of asbestos in the United States, it began selling its stockpiles to countries that did not have comprehensive health and welfare policies.

The underlying theme among each of the arguments listed above is the notion that political behavior is, at its core, unhealthy, counter to organizational goals, and essentially predatory. Writers who have taken this view argue with conviction, that the sooner politics is removed from the organizational arena, the better organizations will be in terms of operations and personal relationships.

In recent years, another school of thought has developed to counter the "negative" school. While not denying the potential for abusing the use of politics through self-serving behavior and subsequently damaging organizational relationships, this second school of thought tends to take a more neutral view of the process. This philosophy contends that politics and political activity are a natural part of organizations and must be acknowledged as no different, in essence, than a firm's culture or organizational structure. This argument further suggests that politics can be neither characterized as good nor bad but rather, as natural and, as such, counters previous arguments by suggesting that efforts or calls to eliminate politics are naive. Politics, this school of thought contends, "exists" and must be learned and applied, preferably in a non-aggressive manner [10, 11, 12, 13].

There are six propositions that underscore the neutral or "natural" view of organizational politics. These propositions follow a logical sequence as they develop the argument for understanding the "true" nature of politics.

**Proposition 1**: Most important decisions in organizations involve the allocation of scarce resources. This statement lays the groundwork under which the context for decision making is established. When decisions need to be made, particularly in the context of group decisions, often they are triggered by some problem or concern. For example, suppose that the operations of a city planning department are fragmented and haphazard. A committee would be tasked with finding ways of reworking operating policies or alternatives for how operations are conducted. The decision they arrive at and, indeed, the decision process itself, is almost always bounded by a number of contingency factors. For example, a short time frame for making the recommendations, a limited operating budget, or the concerns and prerogatives of senior managers may all form a boundary within which the decision must be made. And one of the most compelling boundaries is the scarcity of resources. All organizations, public and private, have limited resources with which to operate. There are limited good jobs to go around. There is only so much money that can be spent. The list is endless. Consequently, any attempts toward arriving at the optimal decision in dealing with a perceived problem are necessarily constrained by the limits of scarce resources.

To take this proposition one step further, not only are virtually all decisions constrained by scarce resources, but the majority of important decisions made within organizations involve, to one degree or another, the allocation or distribution of these scarce resources among a number of competing demands. Departmental budgets are submitted to divide up organizational resources in as equitable and productive a manner as possible. The decision of whether or not to develop and implement a project involves the implicit trade-off between investing in that project and other demands that could be met with the money that was budgeted to initiate the project's development. Consequently, these points give credence to the argument that decision making, particularly important decisions, is in some way bound to the prioritization and distribution of organizational resources.

**Proposition 2**: The decision process often involves bargaining, negotiating, and jockeying for position. It is likely to come as no surprise that the manner by which many decisions are made is often based less on purely logical decision making processes than on a variety of intervening criteria. Certainly, as James March and Herbert Simon noted over 35 years ago, individuals strive for logic in their decision processes. For a variety of reasons, however, we are often more likely to be influenced by and make use of a variety of extra or additional criteria in arriving at decision choices [14]. One process common within organizations where scarce resources are the rule is to make use of bargaining or negotiation behavior. Bargaining follows one of the most common approaches to dealing with conditions of scarce resources, individuals and department heads make deals or compromises between the variety of competing desires and organizational reality. Since all parties cannot attain everything they seek due to scarce resources, to gain as much advantage as possible, individuals who may be in competitive relationships are forced to compromise or negotiate.

**Proposition 3**: Organizations are coalitions composed of a variety of self-interested groups. It is important to understand that when we refer to an "organization" it may be a convenient shorthand to use the term in a monolithic sense; that is, that an organization can and will act as a single, purposeful entity. In reality, the term "organization" gives meaning to the truth behind this misperception. In both the public and private arenas, organizations are composed of a variety of groups: labor vs. management, finance vs. marketing, and so forth. These groups, which must be viewed as essentially self-interested, are the sum of what comprises an organization. This proposition will, on the surface, raise some doubts. For example, the notion these groups are basically self-interested implies a willingness to put their own concerns before the legitimate goals and concerns of the organization. Some may object to this characterization as it implies these groups will seek their own objectives even at the expense of what is best for the organization. In reality, while the different interest groups in the organization generally do buy in to the overall corporate goals, they do so to varying degrees and rarely are willing to ascribe to all of the firm's objectives. The reasons for this reluctance to totally subordinate their own desires to corporate-wide objectives are outlined in proposition 4.

**Proposition 4:** **Groups differ in terms of goals, values, attitudes, time frames, etc.** In 1967, a landmark research study was conducted by Paul Lawrence and Jay Lorsch [15] that sought to investigate the manner in which roles and attitudes differ among various sub-groups in organizations. They uncovered and introduced a phenomenon they referred to as "organizational differentiation." The concept of differentiation was used to describe the fact that as individuals enter the organization, joining a functional group such as accounting or marketing, they develop a set of values and objectives that are in accord with that functional group—that is, they begin to ascribe to sub-group values and attitudes rather than strictly organization-wide objectives. The reasons for this phenomenon are obvious: It is in their functional reference group (marketing, finance, R&D, etc.) that individuals are staffed, given task assignments, evaluated, and rewarded. Hence, their allegiance becomes focused on their immediate work group.

The second important finding of Lawrence and Lorsch was that these functional groups usually differ in terms of a number of important criteria: goals, time frames, values, and so forth. To illustrate, consider the situation often found in organizations having separate R&D and marketing departments. Marketing is primarily concerned with making sales to customers; in fact, the reward systems (bonuses, promotions, and incentives) for those who work in marketing departments are usually geared toward sales volume achieved. Given reward systems that value sales volume, it is easy to understand the emphasis marketing personnel place on short-term profitability and "making their numbers." Compare this value system to that of a typical R&D department where incentives are related to creativity, innovation, and technological development. These activities cannot be regulated in any way that is similar to the approaches used in marketing. Further, the time frames of R&D personnel are often long-term, aimed at achieving technological development. Naturally, the short-term, sales volume goals of marketing not only differ from R&D's long-term focus, but often they actually conflict—that is, in

69

order for marketing personnel to achieve their goals, R&D staff may have to sacrifice theirs.

This is the basic contradiction uncovered by Lawrence and Lorsch that pervades most organizations. Sub-groups within organizations differ due to differences in a variety of criteria: time frames, objectives, attitudes, values, and so forth. The result of this change in goal criteria is why these groups must, to some degree, be characterized as self-interested—feeling most keenly the need to achieve their own departmental objectives first. These differences are important because they shape the types of dynamics that almost always characterize the modern organization.

**Proposition 5:** Because of scarce resources and enduring differences, conflict is central to organizational life. This proposition forms the underlying rationale behind the political model of organizational life. Because of the essential differences and contradictions that exist within organizations, conflict is not simply a side effect of organizational members' interaction, it is a natural and self-perpetuating state. Arguments to the effect that conflict must be eliminated from organizations take a simplistic and exceedingly naive view of the manner in which all organizations operate. Rather than focus on conflict elimination, we are better served to acknowledge its inevitability, its impact, and how we can take steps to channel it appropriately.

**Proposition 6:** Because conflict is inevitable, the use of power and politics becomes a mechanism for resolving conflict situations. Conflict is a natural state within resource-scarce and divergent organizations. Political behavior is an important tool for controlling and resolving conflicts in cost-effective and useful ways. As a result, politics cannot be characterized as malevolent and deviant, but must be seen as a natural consequence of the interaction between organizational sub-systems. This "natural" view of politics refuses to condemn the use of political tactics among organizational members as it views these behaviors as an expected side effect of company life.

# Political Tactics

It is important to consider some of the more common political tactics that occur in organizations. These tactics comprise both negative and natural aspects of politics; some are inherently self-serving and predatory, others are aimed at expanding power or influencing decision processes. In either case, the focus is on attempting to gain a measure of power within the organization. The difference usually is in how this power, once acquired, is used by organizational members.

While there are a wide variety of political tactics that are used to varying degrees within organizations [7], we have focused on some of the more well-known activities. Among the common tactics and political behaviors employed are acts to: (1) expand networks and build coalitions, (2) control decision processes, and (3) develop and project expertise. Expanding networks and building coalitions is one of the most common political behaviors seen in organizations. People who understand and use politics well realize the best way to get what they need is to never force an issue to a head; rather, they are much more likely to network with powerful members of the organization who are able to give them their desired objectives.

Politicians have two reasons for avoiding open fights. First, they realize that when an issue comes to a head publicly, it forces them to defend their actions and views publicly. Politicians, as many of us can attest, prefer to remain in the background while maintaining congenial relations with all because it is in such an atmosphere that they are able to achieve their ends more effectively. The second reason why they prefer to avoid open conflict is that political actors are perfectly willing to target any member of the organization as a potential ally for future actions. The last thing good politicians want is open conflict with another member of the organization because it virtually eliminates a potential source for future favors and advantages.

A far better method of achieving their ends involves the politician working to create and continually expand a network of allies and acquaintances who can be called upon to help when needed. Through networking and developing a widespread coalition, politicians are better able to call in favors or influence decisions involving allocating scarce resources. In discussing the process of coalition building, a senior manager at a company made the powerful statement, "Only an idiot waits for a decision to be made at the meeting." What he was suggesting was that, through networking, a politically savvy individual will have already influenced key decision makers to such a degree that the "meeting" to make the decision is often moot.

Controlling decision processes is the politician's effort to constrain the bounds of a decision in such a way that when the decision is finally made it is in accordance with the politician's wishes. There are several ways to control decision-making processes; some are unethical, others may be considered perfectly legitimate. For example, consider the situation in which a city planning department is planning to purchase a computer system and a member of the department has been tasked with gathering information about various PC-based alternatives. And suppose this individual has a vested financial interest in the selection of one specific vendor. An unethical approach to controlling the decision process would be to present only that information which would validate the politician's choice of computer vendor. In other words, information is held or used selectively in order to guide a decision in a desired direction.

The other method for controlling the decision process is to find ways to influence the meeting agenda or decision-making approaches. For example, suppose the head of a corporate R&D department wished to propose the development of a new, high-technology project. The project's initial investment will be $250,000 and approval for such a project must come from key members of upper management. There are several tactics that could be employed to attempt to influence the decision process. "Sowing" questions, for example, with two or three confederates in the audience during the project proposal, to be asked at key points in the presentation will give the manager the chance to demonstrate knowledge of the system as well as impress the meeting's members with his or her "spontaneous" expertise. And using the meeting agenda itself as an influence tool can be very effective. This process consists of burying a particular issue of concern far down the list of agenda items where it is likely to be quickly dealt with by tired or bored committee members.

The final political tactic is developing and projecting expertise. If others perceive an individual as being an expert on a particular topic, that individual is deferred to and given control. It is important to remember that "expertise" is a perceptual issue. In other words, whether or not an individual truly does have expertise in a particular field is immaterial. What is important is that others believe he or she has expertise. Consequently, a well-known political tactic is to enhance legitimacy and expertise as a method for status. Being the only member of a department to be proficient with the organization's computer equipment guarantees that member a measure of status and power.

An interesting analysis of four megaprojects illustrates the force for good or ill that imagined experts can wield. Two of the projects refer to civil aircraft development (Concorde and Airbus) and two are space agencies (ESRO and ELDO). The two successful projects (Airbus and ESRO) were found to be comparable in terms of organizational features, whereas the two less successful (a euphemism for "disaster") were similar with respect to their organizational design. In the first two, professional engineers having real expertise were in charge, they had the power to implement decisions and emerged as champions. In the case of the two project failures, top management was seen as more highly involved in internal politics and projected "imagined expertise." Two quotations regarding the Concorde debacle aptly sum up the analysis, particularly in relation to the success of Airbus.

*"Concorde was an entirely political aeroplane: the plane was to show that we were good Europeans"*

*"After Concorde, an engineer's dream built by politicians, comes Airbus, a businessman's dream built by engineers"* [16]

> *Sir Richard Way*
> Permanent Secretary, British Ministry of Aviation

Obviously, where engineers succeeded, politicians and illusory "experts" failed. In the successful projects, the respective project managers were fully in charge, with decentralized decision-making authority and an absence of constraining bureaucracy. In the absence of strategic vision, leadership, positive incentives, and rapid decision-making processes, as in the cases of Concorde and ELDO, they are bound to fail [17].

## chapter 5

# How You Will Become a Victim of Politics

I
n presenting both the "negative" and "natural" sides of the debate on the nature of corporate politics, it is important for individuals to draw their own conclusions about the role of politics in organizational life. As shown in Table 5.1 people entering organizational service for the first time are likely to take one of three distinct positions regarding political behavior. The first approach can be best termed the "naive" attitude regarding politics. Naive individuals view politics as unappealing at the outset and make firm resolution never to engage in any type of behavior that resembles political activity. Their goal is, in effect, to remain above the fray, not allowing politics in any form to influence their conduct.

The second, and exact opposite, approach is undertaken by individuals who enter organizations with the express purpose of using politics and aggressive manipulation to reach the top. These people are "sharks." While relatively few in number, these people readily embrace political behavior in its most virulent form. Their loyalty is entirely to themselves and their own objectives. Work with them, and one is likely to be used and manipulated; get between them and their goal and their behavior becomes utterly amoral. The only cause these individuals espouse is their own. The "naive" and "shark" positions are equally and unprofitably wrong-minded about politics. Their attitudes underscore the awareness of the third type of organizational actor: the "politically sensible."

Politically sensible individuals enter organizations with few illusions about how many decisions are made. They understand,

**Table 5.1**  Characteristics of Political Behaviors

| Characteristics | Naive | Sensible | Shark |
|---|---|---|---|
| Underlying Attitude— "Politics is ..." | Unpleasant | Necessary | An opportunity |
| Intent | Avoid at all costs | Used to further department's goals | Self-serving and predatory |
| Techniques | Tell it like it is | Network, expand connections, use system to give and receive favors | Manipulation, use of fraud and deceit when necessary |
| Favorite Tactics | None, the truth will win out | Negotiation, bargaining | Bullying, misuse of information, cultivate and use "friends" and other contacts. |

either intuitively or through their own experience and mistakes, that politics is simply another side, albeit an unattractive one, of the behavior in which one must engage in order to succeed in modern organizations. While not shunning politics, neither do they embrace its practice. Rather, the politically sensible are apt to state that this behavior is at times necessary because "that is the way the game is played." It is also important to point out that politically sensible individuals generally do not play politics of a predatory nature, as in the case of sharks who seek to advance their own careers in any manner that is expedient. Politically sensible individuals use politics as a way of making contacts, cutting deals, and gaining power and resources for their departments or projects to further corporate, rather than entirely personal, ends.

Everyone must make up their own minds regarding the efficacy and morality of engaging in corporate politics. Interviewing successful project managers would show it is almost impossible to be successful in organizational systems without a basic understanding of, and willingness to employ, organizational politics. Whatever position one adopts, research has led to some important conclusions about politics. A recent large-scale study of senior and mid-level managers offered a number of interesting conclusions about the use of politics in organizations:

1. While unable to agree whether politics is a natural process, most managers regard politics in a negative manner and view political behavior as unprofitably consuming organizational time and resources.

2. Managers believe political behavior is common to all organizations.

3. The majority of managers believe political behavior is more prevalent among upper managers than those at lower levels in organizations.

4. Political behavior is much more common in certain decision domains, such as structural change or new system implementation, than in other types of organizational activities, such as handling employee grievances [1].

The fourth conclusion is particularly relevant to a discussion of corporate politics. The reason political behavior is more common under certain conditions such as new system introduction is that these types of organizational changes signal the potential for a significant shift in power relationships. Any form of organizational change has the potential to alter the power landscape. The reason, as Hickson and his colleagues have noted, is that one important determinant of power is the notion of centrality [2]. Centrality refers to how involved or central to the main activities of an organization a particular individual or department is. The more central to the organization's mission, the greater the power held by that department. The initiation and implementation of a new project has the potential to remove the power of centrality from departments and transfer it to another location—the project team. As previously noted, if a project is developed under the auspices of one department, other functional areas may view that development with suspicion because it shifts the spotlight from their own activities to a project team sitting outside of their jurisdiction. Any action or change effort initiated by members of an organization that has the potential to alter the nature of current power relationships provides a tremendous impetus for political activity.

Why is the study of politics so important for successful project implementation? The implementation process itself is often highly politicized, as different managers and departments view the development and implementation of a project as a potentially useful base of power. In other words, any shift in the operational status quo, resulting from the introduction of a new project within a corporation, will inevitably affect how operations and activities are conducted. Once there is a threatened shift in status, departments and managers who perceive themselves as losing power because of the project are apt to do whatever is necessary to discourage or subvert its use.

Consider a situation in which a city planning department has contracted to install an MIS with the technical ability to perform a wide variety of tasks, including infrastructure tracking and repair, tasks originally handled by the city engineering department. As a result of the new MIS the city planners have the capacity to track and schedule road and bridge repair themselves. Under this scenario, one would expect the city engineers to do everything they can to either halt use of the MIS or severely limit it in such a way that it will not interfere with activities they view as their responsibility. For example, they might push through a procedural resolution requiring all infrastructure repair planning be done through their office, despite the existence of the MIS. The conclusion is inescapable: with responsibility comes power. If the computer system reallocates operational responsibilities, it thereby redefines the power structure. Few changes are as threatening to organizational members as a redivision of power. Hence, those with a vested interest in the old system will actively resist efforts to introduce new or innovative changes.

## Political Games

The number of political games played within organizations are legion. Some are entirely predatory and others are relatively benign. This chapter, indeed this book, is in no way intended to advocate employing predatory political practices as a means to advancing selfish or egocentric ends. Nevertheless, as firm believers in the adage, "Forewarned is forearmed," we offer the following analysis of political practices so that project managers can: (1) learn to recognize political games when they are the target, and (2) develop and employ political tools as appropriate in furthering their project's legitimate ends.

Harrison [3] developed a set of political principles he labeled the political manager's tool kit. His list is broad and offers a fine framework for a more in-depth discussion of various political tactics. He cites a set of ten activities that are political in nature and can work to a manager's advantage if employed prudently. Not all of the tactics are savory, nor are they all recommended for use. Nevertheless, as a starting point for understanding the types of political games prevalent in modern organizations, each offers a clear window for examining the political realm (see Table 5.2). The ten political tools are:

1. Gaining support from a higher power source or sources
2. Alliance or coalition building
3. Controlling a critical resource
4. Controlling the decision process
5. Controlling the committee process
6. Use of positional authority
7. Use of the scientific element
8. Deceit and deception
9. Information
10. Miscellaneous games.

**Gaining support from a higher power source or sources.** All projects proceed more smoothly if they can attract the sponsorship of a powerful champion. Rather than passively waiting and hoping a champion will appear and aid the project, smart politics suggests project managers should go out and actively enlist support. Some of the methods used to gain support include the sponsorship game, lobbying, and co-optation. Sponsorship refers to any attempts that a junior manager makes to get a senior manager to "sign on" and mentor the project. Lobbying is often seen as the visible manifestation of such attempts. A project manager may work to advertise his project in any organizational circles he can find, using such publicity as a jumping off point for directly approaching a senior manager. Co-optation is the project manager's practice of employing allies in the search for a champion. Rather than act alone, a smart politician will cast a wide net, using other managers and additional contacts to single out and approach potential top management supporters.

**Alliance or coalition building.** Alliance or coalition building is a favorite tactic of canny political actors and one of the most common forms of political behavior in organizations. Smart politicians

**Table 5.2**  Political Tactics

1. Gaining support from a higher power source or sources
   - sponsorship
   - lobbying
   - co-optation
2. Alliance or coalition building
   - IOUs
   - deals
   - establish common cause
   - mutual support or defense
3. Controlling a critical resource
   - money
   - people
   - information
   - expertise
4. Controlling the decision process
   - control "short list"
   - control decision criteria
5. Controlling the committee process
   - agenda
   - membership
   - minutes
   - pre-agenda negotiations
   - chairmanship

6. Use of positional authority
   - rewards
   - coercion
7. Use of the scientific element
   - planning
   - control
8. Deceit and deception
   - secrecy
   - surprise
   - hidden agendas
   - hidden objectives
   - two faces
   - all things to all people
9. Information
   - censoring or withholding
   - distortion
10. Miscellaneous games
    - divide and rule
    - whistle blowing
    - in the same lifeboat

Source: F.L. Harrison. 1992. *Advanced Project Management: A Structured Approach*, 3rd Edition. New York: Halstead Press.

recognize that the wider their circle of allies, "friends," and contacts, the greater their potential source of support in times of need. Indeed, bargaining, which forms the basis for much of political behavior, is enhanced by a large coalition. One common method for developing alliances include giving and accepting of IOUs. Many times it is in a manager's best interest to perform a favor for another; not for immediate gain but in order to be able to call in a marker in the future if it should be necessary. Likewise, canny politicians learn the art of negotiation and dealmaking as natural byproducts of their profession.

Other forms of alliance building include "treaties" of mutual support and defense and establishing common causes. It is axiomatic that clever politicians couch their approach and request for support in terms of appeals to the higher good. This approach has many benefits, perhaps the most obvious of which is that, if done properly, it reframes the issue at hand as one of mutual interest rather than self-interest. In other words, if a politician can convince others that it is in their best interest to perform some task he personally desires, the politician benefits doubly: (1) through getting others to help fight his battles, while (2) not having to owe favors in return. As an illustration of this principle, a large business school recently undertook a major revision of their curriculum in order to weed out old, nonessential courses and update the teaching approach. The head of one department, facing severe cuts, managed to convince the heads of two other departments that the revision would damage their prerogatives as well. Although untrue, the politician was thus able to enlist the active and vocal support of other members of the college and ultimately minimize potential damage to his own department.

**Controlling a critical resource.** The ability to control a critical resource is key to developing a base of power. In the days of the Old West, rival cattle barons often fought each other over water and land grazing rights, the two critical resources to support their livelihood. The implication was, and is, clear: "If I can control your access to a resource that is critical to your operations, I win." In project management situations, one of the most obvious sources of power disequilibrium is the control that managers have over the work of their subordinates, often requiring project managers to negotiate for services they need performed. Other critical resources that project managers seek, but which are in short supply, include money, expertise, and relevant and timely information.

**Controlling the decision process.** A subtle but effective political tactic involves the capacity to control organizational decision processes. There are two variations on this tactic. In the first, the canny political manager will work to control the selection of options to a final "short list" to ensure his preferences are included while stacking the deck with other, unacceptable options. Consider, for example, a project manager seeking to have another technical expert assigned to the project team. He may approach upper management with a short list of alternates, knowing in advance that other commitments will prevent some of the undesirable alternatives from being selected. Nevertheless, for appearance's sake, the manager has given the impression of having no hidden agenda or particular preference, while actually working carefully to ensure his preferred choice is selected.

Another method for controlling the decision process involves controlling the decision criteria themselves. In this scenario, politicians understand a decision must be made which, although they may have no power to do so, they would like to personally influence. In controlling the decision criteria, the politician may seek to constrain the boundaries of the decision to limit the information search and "force" a committee or upper manager to arrive at a decision the politician is actively pushing. In one case, for example, a manager has a vested financial interest in a multimillion-dollar purchase of personal computers for a large corporate office. In an effort to influence the selection, competition among three top contenders was set in terms of carefully selected performance criteria, knowing that these were the few areas in which his choice was demonstrably better. Not surprisingly, his choice won.

**Controlling the committee process.** We like to think most important decisions are made by objective committees in which the logic of consensus operates. Many times nothing could be further from the truth. That sounds harsh but it must be put into its proper context. Committees, first and foremost, are composed of individuals with their own likes and dislikes, biases, and personal agendas. They sometimes function in ways that do not maximize the organization's return but rather protect their own power. Committees, and meetings in general, are often a sore point for project managers who find themselves spending large amounts of time in rounds of discussions that seem to generate little positive return. Nevertheless, meeting skills are critical because they are still the standard for significant decision-making in most organizations.

Politicians understand committees serve a purpose but they also seek to find ways to influence the committee's oversight or to ensure that the committee arrives at the same decision the manager has already reached. There are several ways to influence committee decision-making. The most important, and often overlooked, is by "allowing" the committee to make the decision in the first place. Why wait until the meeting and pin your hopes on a favorable outcome if you have the opportunity to influence each committee member prior to the meeting? Alternatively, it makes perfect sense to work toward getting the "right" people on the committee in the first place. For example, a particularly successful academic routinely intercedes to salt important committees with his allies, knowing he will need their support at appropriate times. It makes more sense to manage the decision through controlling the committee process.

Other methods for controlling the committee process include approaches that manipulate the agenda or committee membership. For example, a senior manager was known for an autocratic style until being warned to become more "team-oriented" in decision-making. The solution? Find four staff members that he knew he could always count on to do his bidding and consistently staff committees with these individuals. The illusion of team decision-making masked the manipulation of the committee through careful staffing.

Finally, beware of the truly manipulative politicians who seek to control committees by altering meeting minutes after the fact. Though this tactic is somewhat rare, it can be highly damaging. Few of us actually read minutes of old meetings we have attended. Politicians know this and sometimes make subtle alterations to the intended meaning of group decisions if given the opportunity. In one case, a manager who had been altering meeting minutes for years was finally caught. He had discovered he was the only one who kept copies of the minutes and when, in the course of his job, he made mistakes, he would alter the minutes to seemingly pass the blame on to other managers. Admittedly, this example is an extreme case but nevertheless offers a particularly ruthless example of the use and misuse of information.

**Use of positional authority.** While not a formal political tactic, positional authority gives managers an important base of power and influence. It is not typically considered a "political" approach because positional authority, by definition, relies on legitimate power for control; hence, there is little need to engage in the sorts of influential activities political realities necessitate. On a larger scale, however, one could argue that having some specific base of authority gives project managers a component of status vis-à-vis functional managers and other important stakeholders, enabling them to negotiate and operate on more equal footing. In many corporations, for example, project managers have relatively little status or authority, being named to their position on an ad hoc or "availability" basis. Is it any wonder they are forced to work through influence and similar "powerless" approaches to further their project's goals? Contrast this situation to organizations that are project-based (e.g., Boeing or Fluor Daniel). These firms quite literally live and die by project management. Consequently, the title of "project manager" carries with it enough status and positional authority to make it easy for these people to negotiate with peers and punish or reward their subordinates.

**Use of the scientific element.** This political tactic means having the expertise to be knowledgeable on various technical components of the project management process, including the planning and control processes. As noted, an important source of power lies in being perceived as an expert by other organizational and project team members. Developing a reputation as an expert is another method for enhancing authority, although from personal rather than positional power.

**Deceit and deception.** Some might cynically note no discussion of politics is complete without making mention of its darker side: the overt or (more often) covert manipulation of others in a self-serving manner.

The use of deceit and deception is a political tactic played most often by predatory managers. It is important, however, for other project managers to recognize some of the signals of these games to prepare for their effects and consider reasonable alternative responses. One of the most common forms of deceit and deception is the surprise tactic—the enlistment of an ally and then a sudden move against that person when they least expect it. Other tactics include hidden objectives and agendas and chameleon-like changeability. Deceitful politics breeds shifty actors adept at refusing to allow themselves to be pinned down to any position. They avoid direct conflict because it could create bad feelings and open hostility, preferring to work behind the scenes to gain advantage and eliminate opposition.

Deceitful political actors offer an unsettling message. Unlike many other political tactics, benign or malicious, which are readily identifiable, deception and deceit are, by definition, very difficult to detect prior to implementation. This tactic is much harder to anticipate and defend against because it forces project managers to be somewhat guarded of whom they take into their confidence. This should not be interpreted as an injunction to never trust anyone within the organization. Clearly, project managers need their support group and allies in order to implement their projects. We must be aware, however, of those who operate in essentially unprincipled ways and of the impact they can have on us and our careers. The good news is that there are relatively few Machievellian managers who practice this sort of tactic. The bad news is that once having come across one, it is best to keep a wide distance from them in the future.

**Information.** Those who have information have an advantage over others who need that information to more effectively do their jobs. In playing information politics, probably the most common approach is withholding information that could either reflect badly on individuals or projects. More malicious examples of information politics include the deliberate distortion of information. As information technology becomes more prevalent across organizations, however, this political tactic is increasingly rare. With a number of new sources of almost any form of information available to managers, there is little advantage in distorting information that can easily be cross-checked through another source.

**Miscellaneous games.** James Clavell's novel, *Shogun*, offers some wonderful examples of political maneuvering. Set in feudal Japan, a principle character, Toranaga, had been isolated by the ruling council of regents and condemned. He realized he stood no chance in defying and fighting a united council so he began a series of tactics bent on dividing, one by one, the regents from each other. His policy of divide and rule is a well-known political ploy, used to slowly eliminate the power of a coalition. In a project management example, a manager with a large chemical manufacturing firm was faced with the potential canceling of her project by an oversight group that included representatives from accounting, production, and R&D. She knew she stood virtually no chance of changing the minds of the committee as a whole, so she began working behind the scenes, person by person, trying to convince each one to allow the project to continue. Her favorite tactic was to play on the natural animosities that often exist between members of different departments, in this case R&D and production. She was successful in driving a wedge between the representatives and thereby hamstringing the oversight committee.

Other tactics are well-known: threats of whistle-blowing and appeals for unity in the face of external threats—"We are all in the same lifeboat"—are examples of the range of options in the political manager's toolbox. An in-depth understanding of the choices available to use or be wary of can serve to help project managers better grasp the nature of power and politics in their organizations. And most of us will gravitate toward benign politics, played with the best interests of the organization and the project at hand.

## Summary

Politics is a process few managers, even those who are adept at it, enjoy. Interviews and conversations with a variety of managers across a diverse collection of public and private organizations make clear that using politics, even in the "sensible" manner suggested in this chapter, is often a distasteful process. We do not like having to cut deals, to negotiate for resources needed to develop our projects, and to constantly mollify departmental heads who are suspicious of the motives behind a developing project, or any other system that threatens their base of power. Nevertheless, the realities of modern organizations are such that successful managers must learn to use the political process for their own purposes. This chapter laid out some of the major issues in organizational politics, its definitions and causes, and suggested some guidelines for effectively managing project implementation within the political context of organizations. It also offered some practical views on the nature and importance of political behavior in modern organizations.

## chapter 6

# Project Management Politics: Some Real-World Examples

This chapter contains some examples of the wide variety of political activities that continually occur in organizations. While not intended to be anywhere near a comprehensive list of such behaviors, each example serves to give readers an idea of the wide-ranging nature of political behavior. Although these are true stories, the names of the key players and their organizations have been disguised. The stories stand on their own merits and, although the background data has been changed, readers will quickly see that the message remains the same.

## Story One:
## The Untrustworthy Project Manager

A systems development manager for a large Silicon Valley computer firm was given a new project to oversee. The project consisted of creating a new protocol for integrating computer systems and programs from across the various divisions to develop a uniform reporting and control procedure. The project manager, Neil, had been angling for this assignment for the past three months, knowing it had high visibility and, if performed well, would enhance his career with the company. Neil's managerial style was still developing as he had only been with the company for a little over two years. In that time he had compiled a solid, if unspectacular, performance record and reasoned that successfully steering a couple of high-profile projects to completion would give him a leg-up for promotion.

As part of initial project preparation, Neil began assembling his core project team, composed of other mid-level managers from a variety of functional disciplines. The core team consisted of an MIS representative, two managers from software engineering, one from diagnostics, and one from accounting. After holding a preliminary get-acquainted meeting with the team as a whole, he scheduled a series of one-on-one meetings with each of the core team members. The two representatives from software engineering, Sue and Dan, had almost identical records of service with the company, each having five years in their respective positions.

Neil's meeting with Sue included dialogue along the following lines:

Neil: "Sue, I want you to know that your contribution and commitment will be vital if this project is to succeed. I know that you have put in for that job of senior manager for systems analysis and I've been told by upper management that I can make some promotion recommendations for the top project team performers. It could be the boost you need to make senior manager."

Sue: "That would be great, Neil! You can count on my support 100 percent."

Naturally, Sue left her meeting with Neil highly motivated to do a good job on the project. After all, he had practically promised her a promotion if she pulled her weight on the team. Unbeknownst to Neil—Sue, Dan, and the other three core member members set up an informal get-together over lunch to plot out some issues for coordinating their work. In the course of their meeting, Ira, from accounting, leaned across the lunch table and casually asked Sue, "So, what did Neil promise you when we finish?"

Sue replied, "He promised that he would put me up for senior manager for systems analysis."

Dan's jaw dropped as he leaned across the table and asked, "At which site?"

Sue, puzzled by Dan's reaction, said, "Here."

At this point, Dan's face turned bright red as he began cursing Neil, the project, the company, and anything else he could think of.

Can you guess what had happened? Neil had promised the same promotion to both Dan and Sue. As the team members started comparing notes, they realized Neil had made several promises he either could not keep or, more likely, had no intention of trying to keep.

In the space of that hour-long lunch meeting, the motivation level of each of the core team members plummeted. After all, what was the potential payoff for doing outstanding work? Neil's attempts at influencing and manipulating his team had been discovered and his credibility was immediately ruined. The results were predictable. With the half-hearted support of the project team, Neil's project continued on well past its due date, chewing up additional resources and showing no signs of improvement until upper management grew weary of his excuses and removed him from the team. With his removal, the systems integration project was given to a senior manager who brought it on line in less than two months. To this day, Neil most likely has no idea where the process went wrong.

Neil's story illustrates an important concept in the use of power and influence: the importance of maintaining credibility. Nothing is as difficult to maintain as a reputation for honesty, and once having been undermined, it is almost impossible to rebuild. In Neil's zeal to get his team fired up, he made several promises he had no authority to make, particularly offering the same promotion to two team members. The moral of this story is clear: maintain credibility. Another way of saying this is: "Never promise something you cannot deliver and always deliver on your promises." As a form of influence, a reputation for being a "straight shooter" can be invaluable. Likewise, having the reputation as a liar can ruin a project manager's chances for developing a consistent base of power in any organization.

## Story Two: The Office Bully

A division of a large heavy construction company was set up with a project matrix structure. One of the mid-level managers, Hal, had been with the company for 15 years, performing as a project engineer on a number of industrial construction project teams. Hal's performance had always been marginal. For years, he seemingly did just enough to get by but had a way of wiggling off the hook when project activities for which he was responsible came in late or needed additional resource support. Hal's technique is simple: he makes sure that his engineering team always includes a young engineer who can be easily dominated. As a result, he is able to point to a convenient scapegoat when problems occur, convincing the junior member of the team the problems must, somehow, really be his fault. In this way, Hal has managed to consistently deflect blame from himself for problems while making sure to garner any accolades for successful performance.

Hal's system finally hit a brick wall when he selected a new engineer, Gwen, for a recent international project. Although Hal did not realize it, Gwen made a habit of keeping copies of all internal office communications in a file. Over the course of the 18-month project, she was able to build up quite a large dossier on the project, including memos and meeting minutes between herself and her immediate boss, Hal.

During the transfer phase of the turnkey project, problems started occurring with several key features, prompting the client to issue an urgent call to the company to send people to the site to fix the problems. The on-site inspection revealed several key mistakes in basic engineering design that, to fix, would set the project's transfer back almost six months. Naturally, once this news reached the home organization, there was an in-house investigation into the cause of the errors. Hal immediately reverted to form and indicated Gwen was at fault for the design errors. He then scheduled an appointment with Gwen to, in effect, pin the blame on her and assign her to correct the errors.

Gwen showed up for the meeting lugging a large folder. Hal immediately launched into his favorite political routine, covering himself through passing the blame. In the midst of his tirade, Gwen calmly interrupted him and noted that Hal had been the person responsible for the design errors. Hal angrily replied that she was wrong and started to warm up to his theme again. Without another word, Gwen reached into her folder and pulled out a 14-month-old memo that spelled out individual responsibilities, clearly naming Hal as the person responsible for the design. When Hal attempted to brush the memo aside as inconsequential, Gwen began pulling out other documentation that made it obvious where the fault lay. Hal saw he was beaten and ended the meeting, trying to think of another person on whom to pin the blame.

This story offers an interesting twist to any discussion of political behavior: how to defend yourself against someone attempting to play the blame game at your expense. One of the best defenses to maintain is adequate and comprehensive documentation. This means keeping memos, copies of meeting minutes, upper management directives, and any other internal communications from project team members or relevant stakeholders. Many politicians flourish because they are able to operate with a kind of impunity; that is, freedom from scrutiny or having their activities too closely analyzed. Nothing frightens manipulative politicians quite as much as having their behavior documented. One clue that many of us receive but rarely note about predatory sharks is their unwillingness to commit themselves to paper. "Oh, we don't need to write this up," "You can trust me to keep my word," and "Why hang on to all that old paper, it just clutters up your office" are all phrases repeated again and again by manipulators who have no desire to have their activities documented.

Some readers are uncomfortable with this point. "What are we supposed to do, suspect the motives of everyone we come into contact with?" the unaware may ask. The response is that maintaining documentation does not presume suspicion, it is simply sound business practice. Most project managers routinely keep any documents related to the project's development because all this information may be useful at some point, perhaps during negotiations with clients or upper management. It is equally appropriate and not unusual to keep records of anything concerning your responsibilities or activities on the project. It is a purely defensive maneuver that may never be needed. On the other hand, it could just save your career. All it takes is one shark and one opportunity.

## Story Three:
## The Squeaky Wheel

Sally and Jim were both managers for new product development at a large manufacturing organization headquartered in the Midwest. Typically, the successful career path within this organization included a stint as project manager for new projects, so these positions were actively sought and highly competitive. As a result of the 1991 economic downturn, the top management of the organization circulated a memo indicating they would be developing a cost-control task force to examine each new or ongoing project to ensure that they were offering substantial profit opportunities and were cost-effective.

Most project managers interpreted this memo, correctly, as a potential ax with which to chop off nonperforming projects.

The departments Sally and Jim worked for had seven projects on the drawing board or in various stages of development. The consensus around the department, confirmed informally by their boss, was that in all likelihood either Sally or Jim's project would be eliminated and its personnel reassigned or terminated. Sally and Jim both received notification of a project review meeting to take place the following Friday. The memo further identified key management staff that would be attending and would, most likely, have the final say about termination decisions.

In the week before the Friday meeting, Jim met with his project team and developed a sales pitch to demonstrate why his project had the best long-term benefits to the company. He spent the week getting his records in order and preparing for the fateful meeting.

Sally's approach was very different. Armed with the information about who would be sitting in on the meeting, Sally spent the week seeing each member of the cost control team. With some, she made deals, "Support me on this one and I won't forget it." With others, she used her contacts to act as go-betweens. In each case, Sally found a way to cut a private agreement or develop an understanding prior to the meeting.

Guess who retained funding for their project? If you answered Sally, you are correct. The moral of this story is simple, but important: most important decisions are made before the meeting takes place. Many of us assume a decision-making meeting does just that (i.e., makes a decision). Corporate reality is often vastly different. The manager who naively waits until the actual meeting, believing that he can make his best pitch within the conference room and win the day will always lose to the cannier manager who has been working behind the scenes prior to the meeting. A simple reality of politics is that it involves bargaining and making precisely the sorts of deals that Sally did. Her behavior is not underhanded, it is simply effective and knowledgeable politics.

Some may wonder, is this approach "fair" to those of us who do play by what we perceive are the rules? Is Sally simply perverting the system to her advantage? Those who ask these questions need to consider what lurks behind them. Sally adopted a different strategy than did Jim. Should this decision have been settled in the meeting in some "fair" fashion? Consider that, in responding "yes," one might just as reasonably ask whether or not it is fair that the person who is best at delivering a sales presentation should win, regardless of the relative merits of the two projects. Sally understood a basic rule of organizational life: The squeaky wheel will get the lion's share of the grease.

## Story Four:
## Nothing Succeeds Like Success

Stu Robinson had just finished a program review meeting with the vice president for new product development at a medium-sized computer manufacturer in Northern California. Stu held the title of senior program manager with the organization. In this capacity, a position he had held for four years, Stu was responsible for managing a series of hardware development projects. Stu's record had been steadily successful since his early days as a junior project manager in hardware engineering. As a reward for his ability to bring projects successfully to market, he had received his most recent promotion to senior program manager. He was, in effect, now a manager of project managers.

His recent meeting with the vice president was necessitated by the repeated delays in a new project, one that Stu was not personally responsible for. The project, a high-speed notebook computer using the latest in hardware architecture, had been initiated by the CEO, who created a stand-alone "skunkworks" project team that reported directly to him without any intermediate oversight or reporting steps. The theory behind the move was that it would speed up coordination time and ensure that resources would flow directly to the project as they were needed without jumping through bureaucratic hoops. As a result, the project, assigned to one of the CEO's engineering favorites, was given a mandate to move quickly to marketplace, hopefully within 18 months from project kickoff. That was over two and a half years ago.

The problems encountered by the project were, in many ways, typical of those found with many R&D projects. The notebook computer was intended to exploit new and groundbreaking technologies while maintaining affordability and ease of use. Rather than attempting to introduce its computer into the marketplace with one or perhaps two innovative ideas, the company opted to use this new product as the basis for creating a new generation of computer technology, specifying eight separate and challenging upgrades over the current state-of-the-art notebook computer.

In hindsight, the seeds of some of the biggest problems with the project were sown during its initial conceptualization and project kickoff. First, because the project was the apple of the CEO's eye, he was determined to maintain close contact with the project team and manager, requiring progress reports bimonthly. He also made it clear he expected significant advancement in the project's progress to be demonstrated at each of these meetings. The second serious problem occurred in project manager selection. In picking one of his favorites to head the development team, the CEO made his choice more on the basis of personality compatibility than experience or competency. Certainly, the project manager talked a good game and had some successes on his record, but the general consensus around the engineering department was that he made his reputation on the back of his subordinates. He was notorious for being quick to take praise for successes and equally quick to push blame for problems downhill.

A final problem with the development process was the manner in which it was presented to the various functional department heads who were expected to contribute resources as needed. In general, they felt they were presented with a *fait accompli* in the project, with little input solicited regarding the development schedule, features, or market opportunities that the computer project would present. Marketing, in particular, was less than enthusiastic about the chances for success of the project, reasoning that such a leap in technology as this product represented was bound to be accompanied by design flaws and technical bugs, similar to those experienced by the first Apple Newtons introduced. Instead, they argued for a more incremental development process, through adopting one or two of the technical improvements and establishing a market for the product. Their objections were routinely overridden by the CEO, who insisted that the design be adopted as he initially conceived it.

The project manager, Wesley, encountered problems almost from the beginning from a variety of sources. First, because his technical reputation within engineering was not particularly strong, he sought to enhance the team by drafting the best and brightest from the hardware engineering department. His autocratic and rather arrogant style quickly alienated the head of hardware engineering who perceived that the loss of his best design personnel would seriously compromise the other work of his functional group. His objections to the CEO were routinely overridden and he was ordered to comply with Wesley's "requests." From that point on, the head of hardware engineering began waging a surreptitious guerrilla war against Wesley and the notebook project, talking the project down at every opportunity and hiding funding and personnel from Wesley's view. Although perhaps not as severe, similar stories were encountered within other departments as Wesley seemed to revel in his abrasive management style.

An additional problem had its roots in the CEO's insistence that each project review meeting was expected to demonstrate measurable progress. Consequently, Wesley made two serious mistakes. First, he started "fudging" the data he submitted to the CEO, offering evidence of greater progress than the team was actually achieving and minimizing design or engineering problems, in spite of the incredible technical challenges the project represented. Second, out of fear that he had to show immediate results, Wesley spent almost no up-front time with scheduling, risk analysis, scope management, or any of the other necessary preliminary project management steps. Indeed, his Work Breakdown Structure (WBS) was so cursory as to be almost useless, specifying steps and budget lines at such a general level of detail that they were quickly shown to be unrealistic. It became a dictum of Wesley's project to always show results, even if illusory, and never discuss setbacks, even if unforeseen.

The results of these errors in judgment had immediate and far-reaching effects on the company. Originally budgeted for slightly less than four million dollars in R&D funding, the project continued to roll up enormous deficits, especially when department heads began using the project to hide some of their own overruns. Technically, the project never seemed to get out of first gear, particularly in terms of rework cycles. A common project work progression had first the designs and later the prototypes move linearly through a series of functional activities. First, product design would develop some blueprints which were then shipped "over the wall" to engineering who would critique the designs and specify necessary changes. After several cycles from design to engineering and back, designs would then be sent to production for their input, almost always necessitating another round of design changes as production offered several limitations from a manufacturing viewpoint. After a seemingly interminably process, consensus was finally reached on prototype development. These rework cycles were variously estimated to have consumed anywhere from 6–12 months of the project.

Approximately 15 months into the project, it finally became clear to the CEO that he had been receiving overly rosy reports from his original project manager. He then decided on a major housecleaning, in which the project manager, head project engineer, and project administrator were all replaced. The result of this ax-wielding only seemed to push the project further behind. Meanwhile technical and coordination problems continued to beset the project as the new leadership team was brought up to speed and attempted to develop working ties with the functional departments. After another six months, the second project manager, showing little additional improvement, was replaced by a third project manager. Since then, almost a year has passed, the project is still in prototype and despite frequent pronouncements from the CEO, costs are climbing and schedules continue to slip. Perhaps worst of all, the project is acquiring the reputation as a "career buster," as personnel continue to turn over while the project staggers on.

It was with this backdrop that Stu Robinson was appointed the fourth project manager with broad powers to get the computer to market while there was still any kind of window of opportunity. Taking stock of his task, Stu began underlining some of the key problems with the project as he perceived them. First, it was clear that initial time frames were unrealistically optimistic. Too much new or cutting-edge technology was being married too quickly without working out technical bugs and likely misfit problems. Schedules had never incorporated the necessary time to ensure that the technology was working correctly. A second problem had to do with the CEO's direct involvement in the development. Certainly, Stu reflected, it helps any project to have direct support from the head of the company, but the CEO's help had instead become a hindrance. He insisted on rapid progress without allowing for sufficient up-front planning. Further, he had routinely ordered technical upgrades as new computer breakthroughs occurred, preventing the project team from ever being able to lock-in to a set of specifications. The sum total of the CEO's activities had actually delayed the project and pushed it over budget.

Stu also realized that bridges would have to be rebuilt between the project team and the various functional groups, particularly hardware engineering. Constant sniping by these department heads had a significant and unwelcome effect on team morale, particularly as they felt themselves pulled in two different directions by dual loyalties: the project and their functional departments.

Armed with considerable leeway to bring the project back from nearly dead, Stu immediately suspended project operations pending a series of extensive program review meetings. In these meetings, Stu made it clear that he was not sent in to kill the project but to try and save it. At the same time, he formalized various roles to prevent overlap, made a preliminary decision to freeze specifications in place, pending approval from the CEO, and revamped the planning mechanisms for greater detail and job responsibility specification. Next, he met with the CEO and was able to make the case to lock-in specifications without significant changes while making clear to top management the steps he deemed appropriate to get the project back on track.

Stu's next move was extremely important: he scheduled a series of meetings with the various department heads to inform them of his appointment to the project. Because Stu had a good working relationship with these individuals (something he had been careful to cultivate during his time with the company), he was able to secure their cooperation and active support. He was even able to bring the head of hardware engineering, despite his misgivings concerning the project, back into an attitude of compliance. In re-forming these contacts, Stu made use of every political favor he had ever been owed and every close tie he had developed. Further, he willingly cut deals with some of these people, bargaining his future support for their current cooperation.

Stu's technical and political skills began to slowly bear fruit in terms of project improvement. The team stopped receiving mixed messages from their department heads concerning dual loyalties and were able to commit themselves to the project. Further, top management stopped sniping at and attempting to marginalize the project, finally realizing it did have a reasonable chance of capturing significant market share in the computer industry. Finally, the CEO relaxed his reporting requirements following a request by Stu, who had asked to be allowed to run the project without excessive day-to-day top management involvement.

What has been the upshot of Stu's turnaround? While too early to tell how the product will be received in the marketplace, early signs are promising. Certainly, the company learned some valuable and expensive lessons in developing this computer, but whether they will ever earn the kinds of profit margins on it that they had hoped for is unclear. Stu's success came from turning a project around that had been all-but-given-up-for-dead. While he performed a number of separate acts in bringing the project back, it is clear that one of the most impressive and important was his ability to mend fences with the various departments that had become antagonistic because of the political ineptitude of previous project managers.

Is there a moral in this story? Certainly it illustrates another good example of what not to do in managing a project, but more than that, it offers some interesting guidelines on project turnaround. In this case, it is important to acknowledge that turnaround was dependent upon a range of actions taken by Stu, technical and administrative. However, not least among these actions was Stu's acknowledgment that the project stood little chance of success unless he was willing to exert his considerable political talents to rebuild relationships between the project team and the rest of the organization. Stu's story is a classic example of politics in action, not in a negative way, but through accepting that much of what may be necessary to ensure a project's successful introduction goes beyond the realm of the technical into that of the political.

## Summary

These stories are from personal experience and interviews with project managers who, when asked, tell impressive war stories of past project successes and failures. Obviously, it would be a mistake to over-generalize their conclusions to suggest that politics is the overriding cause of project success across all situations and organizations. It is not. On the other hand, a common theme of many failed projects is the political ineptitude of the project manager. All project managers must learn to find ways to extend their power and influence within their organizations if they are to improve the chances of project success. These stories are useful in illustrating some ways in which political prowess can contribute to project success, just as naiveté can often presage problems of a considerable magnitude.

## chapter 7

# Negotiation Skills

**T**his chapter takes an in-depth look at one of the most important and often underused resources in any project manager's toolkit, the process of negotiation. Why include a chapter on negotiation in a book ostensibly aimed at project management power and politics? One of the central points this book makes is that what constitutes a project manager's basis for control lies in his or her ability to use influence well. Because formal power (and its perquisites) is frequently denied them, canny project managers have made their careers out of cultivating and becoming adept at less-formal methods of power, including political behavior and various influence tactics. Negotiation is a process predicated on a manager's ability to use influence and politics productively. The essence of negotiation requires there be no formal method for either side using power for conflict resolution. As a result, the more project managers know about negotiation and the better they become at the process, the greater their influence skills are likely to become.

If we are honest with ourselves, many of us will admit that we are pretty lousy negotiators. We are either impatient, stubborn, narrow-minded, shortsighted, take all objections personally, or some combination of all of these. Americans in particular have developed an unenviably bad reputation as negotiators. Stories to reinforce this seeming inability are legion. For example, the American optical firm that negotiated itself out of several million dollars in licensing fees, because negotiators mistook the silence of their Japanese counterparts following their bid for hostility. It is ironic that we have such a weak reputation when we engage in negotiations daily. Determining mutually agreeable bedtimes with our children, deciding where to go for dinner, and when our teenager must be home are all examples of negotiation.

Project managers, in particular, understand the importance of negotiating skills because so much of their corporate life is spent in negotiations of one type or another. Indeed, some have termed stakeholder management as effective and constant mutual negotiation across multiple parties. Project managers negotiate for additional time and money, to prevent excessive interference and specification changes from clients, important project team personnel, functional managers, and so forth. Negotiation is the art of influence taken to its highest level. Table 7.1 gives five keys to developing a rational, systematic program for negotiating, rather than relying on ad hoc, spur-of-the-moment tactics as we approach each new negotiation.

This chapter develops a systematic program for negotiating. It suggests a framework for better understanding the nature of the negotiation process: Who should be involved? Under what circumstances will negotiation work or not work? What must we keep in mind throughout the negotiation process? All of these questions are fundamental to our becoming better, more influential negotiators.

## When to Negotiate

The first question, "When should we negotiate?" asks us to consider when a negotiation meeting is appropriate to solve inherent differences. There are three primary criteria that must be satisfied for a negotiation to be warranted and potentially fruitful [1]. Briefly, these are when:

- There are no gross power differences.
- You want what they have, and vice versa.
- There are no limiting constraints (e.g., time, geography, legal constraints, competitive information).

The first criterion, no gross power differences, implies two parties enter the negotiation with relatively similar standing; that is, neither party has the ability to hold a gun to the head of the other. For example, many of us feel a "negotiation" between ourselves and the Internal Revenue Service is something less than a fully reasoned or

---

**Table 7.1**  Developing Negotiating Instincts

1. **Avoid Confrontations**—Prematurely digging your heels in encourages the other side to do the same. Keep your options open.

2. **Cast Your Negotiating Team Carefully**—Select the right mix of people for your team. Remember to pick one spokesperson and stick with that person.

3. **Check Your Emotional Baggage at the Door**—Negotiate using reason, not emotion. Keep a close watch on your blood pressure.

4. **Remember the Competition**—Being too intransigent will encourage your opponent to explore other options, including your competitors.

5. **Use Candor**—Nothing is quite so disarming as the willingness to state your position clearly and demonstrate an awareness of the other side's interests.

Adapted from M.H. McCormack. 1989. *What They Still Don't Teach You in Harvard Business School.* New York: Bantam.

---

equitable debate. The IRS has too much power to make more than a token effort at pretending to consider our wishes. Likewise, in the days before baseball free agency, players of even the highest caliber typically had little bargaining power versus the owners who could dictate salaries, bonuses, and working conditions to players who had no choice but to accept them.

In a true negotiation there is no obvious "gross" power differential that would render the negotiation farcical. Rather, both parties have relatively similar standing, such as a project manager and a functional manager who must negotiate a subordinate's work time or a department's logistical support for the project. Under these circumstances, neither party can dictate the process but both must come together to mutually solve a problem or arrive at an agreement.

The second criterion for a negotiation refers to the obvious, both parties have something that the other party seeks. Whether it is money, resources, or the peace and quiet to be left alone, this second criterion adds the value element to the negotiation process. It is only when two parties perceive a sense of value in adopting or seeking the other party's position that there is any motivation to engage in negotiation in the first place. Members of the 1996 Olympic Site Selection Committee, for example, sought a location offering modern amenities, easy access, good infrastructure, sports facilities, and hotels. Atlanta's political and business communities perceived the status of hosting the Summer Olympics in terms of stature and revenues for the city. Both parties clearly had what the other sought, and the negotiations resulted in a mutually satisfactory outcome.

The third criterion refers to limiting characteristics such as time constraints, distance, legal difficulties, and communications snafus. A negotiation, in order to be effective, must be perceived as operating free and clear from any external pressures. Many successful negotiations occur under conditions of relative secrecy, such as settling terms for the acquisition of one company by another. On the other hand, consider one of the standard ploys used by both parties in the 1994 labor negotiations for Major League Baseball. In this case, each side (owners and players) attempted to turn up the heat on the other by implying that if their offers were not accepted by a fixed date, games would not be played. It is instructive to observe the results of these arbitrarily imposed deadlines: In neither case did the other party cave in. Rather, the baseball season was suspended and ultimately canceled.

## Questions to Ask Prior to the Negotiation

Anyone entering a negotiation needs to consider three salient questions prior to adopting a negotiating strategy. These questions are:

1. Power—How much do I have?
2. Time—What sort of pressures are there?
3. Trust—Do I trust my opponent?

The first two questions require a realistic self-assessment concerning power and any limiting constraints, and the answers are absolutely vital prior to sitting down to negotiate. These answers will show the negotiators where they are strong and, most important, where they are weak. A consulting client once related the following story:

"It was early in June and we were involved in the second week of pretty intense negotiations with a vendor for site considerations before starting a construction project. Unfortunately, the vendor discovered that we do our accounting books on a fiscal basis, ending June 30th and he figured, correctly, that we were desperate to record the deal prior to the end of the month. He just sat on his hands for the next ten days. By June 21st and my boss was having a heart attack about locking in the vendor. Finally, we practically crawled back to the table in late June and gave him everything he was asking for in order to record the contract."

This example illustrates the dangers of having an incomplete understanding of factors that can severely limit one's ability to negotiate successfully. How much power do you have going into the negotiation? Remember, one is not necessarily looking for a dominant position but a defensive one; that is, one from which the other party cannot dominate. Likewise, are there any pressing time constraints limiting your freedom to effectively negotiate. The calendar can be difficult to overcome. So, too, can a domineering boss who is constantly saying, "solve the problem with R&D, marketing, or whomever." Once word gets out that there is a time constraint, just watch your opponent slow down the pace, reasoning correctly that you will have to agree sooner rather than later, and to his terms, not yours.

The final and most compelling question to consider is also the most fundamental: Do you trust the other party? Are they people of their word or do they have reputations for changing agreements after the fact? Is their word their bond? Are they forthcoming with accurate information? Do they play hardball in negotiations? Not all of the above questions indicate someone is untrustworthy. Indeed, it is appropriate to play hardball on occasion. The essential question being asked here is whether or not you can sit across a table from your opponent and believe you both have a professional, vested interest in solving a mutual problem in a nonpredatory manner. If the answer is no, it is unlikely that you will negotiate with enthusiasm or openness toward the other party.

Once these three questions have been answered honestly, the chances of engaging in productive and mutually satisfying negotiations are much greater. Figure 7.1 illustrates the starting point from which most negotiations invariably proceed [1]. This figure demonstrates the room for bargaining, the "negotiation space" that exists between two opposing viewpoints. In this case, the negotiation is relatively simple in that it covers one topic: money. The opposing

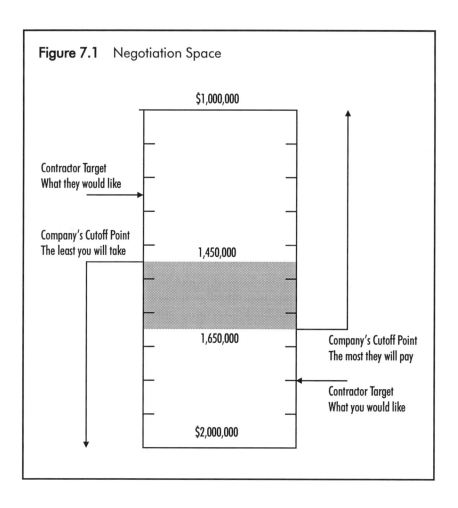

**Figure 7.1** Negotiation Space

$1,000,000

Contractor Target
What they would like

Company's Cutoff Point
The least you will take    1,450,000

1,650,000    Company's Cutoff Point
The most they will pay

Contractor Target
What you would like

$2,000,000

positions held by your company and contractor hinge on determining how much the contractor is willing to pay your company for work to be done. The negotiation space for this particular scenario focuses on your goal of securing as much money as possible from the contractor who, likewise, is interested in paying as little as possible. Certainly, other situations would have more complex negotiating space to take into consideration. This model is instructive, nevertheless, because it is a common situation and will serve as a point of reference to examine some important and useful tips for effective negotiations.

# Tips for Effective Negotiations

One of the most influential books on negotiation in recent years is *Getting to Yes*, by Roger Fisher and William Ury [2]. They offer terrific advice on "principled" negotiation, the art of getting agreement with the other party while maintaining a principled, win-win attitude. Here we offer project managers specific advice on effective negotiating strategies through Fisher and Ury's framework, applying their advice to project-related examples.

## 1. Separate the People From the Problem

One of the most important, profound, and yet common sense ideas of negotiations is just this: negotiators are people first. Negotiators are no different than anyone else in terms of ego, attitudes, biases, education, experiences, and so forth. We all react negatively to direct attacks, we all become defensive at unwarranted charges and accusations, and we, particularly novice negotiators, tend to personalize opposing viewpoints, feeling objections are aimed at us, rather than at the position we represent.

Even the most seasoned negotiators find it difficult to keep cool in the face of withering personal attacks or unfair charges. Consequently, we must seek ways in which we can keep people, their personalities, defensiveness, egos, etc., out of the problem itself. The purpose of negotiation is to fix the problem, not the blame. The more we focus on the issues that separate us and less attention to the people behind the issues, the greater the likelihood of achieving a positive negotiated outcome.

In seeking ways to separate the people from the problem, there are some important guidelines we must consider:

**Put yourself in their shoes.** An old cliché reminds us to never judge another person until you have walked a mile in their shoes. There is a great deal of validity in the notion that we can never come to a meeting of the minds with another party until we consciously consider them and their positions head-on. A great starting point in negotiations is to discuss not only your position but understand the other party's position early in the negotiation process. It has a wonderfully disarming effect on your opponent, entrenched across the bargaining table, when they hear you outline, as objectively as possible, not only your needs but your understanding of their needs as well. When the other party hears a reasoned discussion of both positions, two important events occur: (1) a basis of trust is established because your opponent discovers a willingness to openly discuss perceptions in the beginning, and (2) the negotiation is reconstructed as a win-win, rather than a winner-take-all exercise.

**Don't deduce their intentions from your fears.** A common side effect of almost all negotiations, particularly early in the process, is to construct supporting stereotypes of the other side. We know how this works. When you sit down with the accountant to negotiate additional funding for the project, you invariably adopt a mindset in which all accountants are penny-pinching bean counters who are waiting for the opportunity to pull the plug. But what is happening here? Even before the meeting takes place, you have developed an image of the accounting department and its mindset based on your fears rather than on any objective reality. You assume they will act in certain ways, subconsciously begin negotiating with them as though money is their sole concern, and before you know it, have created an opponent based on your worst fears.

The point is to shed preconceived notions of the character and position of the other party prior to the negotiation. Otherwise the negotiation is likely to begin with a mythical beast representing your worst fears rather than with someone who has a reasonable opposing position. Further, as the negotiation proceeds, you will continue to put the worst possible interpretation on their actions, constantly waiting for the other party to begin to act in ways that support your initial stereotype.

**Don't blame them for your problems.** Blaming is an easy trap to fall into, particularly if you believe the other party is at fault for your difficulties. Nevertheless, in negotiations, it is almost always counterproductive to initiate a finger-pointing episode. Remember, negotiators are people first. When you blame them for your problems, even if you believe it is justified, it only serves to cause them to dig their heels in and become recalcitrant. Find ways to defuse this potential defensiveness. Suppose that a company has just developed a new software program for internal reporting and control that continually crashes. One approach is for the exasperated accounting manager to call in the head of the software development project and chew him out: "Your program really stinks. Every time you claim to have fixed it, it dumps on us again. If you don't get the bugs out of it within two weeks we're going to go back to the old system and make sure that everyone knows the reason why."

While it may be satisfying for the accounting manager to vent his anger like this, it is likely to do little to solve the problem, particularly in terms of relations with the software development project team. A far better approach would have been less confrontational, framing the problem as a mutual issue that needs correction. For example: "The reporting program crashed again in mid-stride. Every time it goes down, my people have to re-input data and use up time that could be spent in other ways. I need your advice on how to fix the problem with the software. Is it just not ready for beta-testing, are we using it incorrectly, or what?" In this case, the head of the accounting department is careful not to point fingers. He refrains from simply setting blame and demanding correction, and instead treats the problem as a problem that will require cooperation if it is to be resolved.

**Recognize and understand emotion—theirs and yours.** It is easy to get emotional during the course of negotiation, but resist the impulse. It is common in a difficult, protracted negotiation for emotions come to the surface. You may be angry or frustrated by the tactics or attitudes of the other party. Nevertheless, it is usually not a good idea to respond in an emotional way, even when the other party becomes emotional. They may be intentionally using emotion as a tactic to get you to lose your cool and allow your heart to guide your head, always a dangerous course. Emotions are a natural side effect of lengthy negotiations. Understand precisely what is making you angry, stressed, or tense. Be astute enough to take note of the emotions emanating from your opponent. And be aware if you are doing something that is making the other person upset or irritable.

A useful technique in negotiation is to allow the other party to let off steam at various times. As a negotiation grows more intense or heated, so too do the emotions of those sitting around the table. Giving your opponent the opportunity to blow up and "tell you off" does not mean you are surrendering anything in terms of the main issues for negotiation. Rather, it is your acknowledgment that other, less seasoned negotiators sometimes react viscerally to continued intransigence. In using a policy of principled negotiation, you are holding out for the best terms you can achieve. So is your opponent. Letting off steam may make it easier to talk rationally later. Further, as a face-saving gesture, the occasional "blow up" can help the other negotiator convince his or her constituency that they are being as tough as they can be, clearing the stage for later, more reasoned discussions.

How are you to react to these blow ups? First, keep your cool. Some negotiators have made a lucrative living out of goading the other party into an exchange of invective, knowing an emotional negotiation is never as productive as a reasoned one. Recognize this tactic. Is your opponent a needler, hoping to find the button that sets you off? If so, you now have an advantage because you recognize their principal negotiating tactic. The story is told of former U.S. Speaker of the House Thomas Reed who was often vilified during Congressional sessions by opponents. Even in the midst of the most inflammatory rhetoric, Reed was never seen to respond with anything other than a grave and formal courtesy. At night, however, after the sessions were finished for the day, he would often sit trembling and red-faced with rage as a result of the emotions that he had managed to keep bottled-up during the day. Remember that the other side has a vested interest in getting and keeping you angry.

**Listen actively.** Active listening means more than sitting quietly and allowing the other party to voice their position. Most of us know from experience when people are really listening to us and when they are simply going through the motions. In the later case, your frustration at their seeming indifference is a tremendous source of negative emotion. For example, consider a client negotiating for a performance enhancement on a soon-to-be-released piece of manufacturing equipment. The project manager wanted to leave the project alone because any reconfigurations at this point would delay the release of the final product. Every time the client voiced their issues, the project manager spoke up and said, "I hear what you're saying, but ..." It quickly became clear the project manager did not, in fact, hear a word the client was saying but was paying lip service to their concerns. Eventually the client went behind the project manager's back to top management and won approval for the specification changes, delaying the project and poisoning the relationship with the project manager and his team.

Active listening means working hard to understand not just the words but the underlying motivations of the other party. One effective technique involves interrupting occasionally to ask a pointed question: "As I understand it, then, you are saying ..." Tactics such as this convince your opponent you are trying to hear what is being said rather than adhering to your company's position no matter what arguments or issues are raised. Demonstrating that you clearly understand the other party's position is not the same thing as agreeing with it. There may be many points with which to take issue. Nevertheless, a constructive negotiation can only proceed from the point of complete and objective information, not from preconceived notions or entrenched and intransigent positions.

**Build a working relationship.** Long-term relationships are key to effective negotiations. Obviously, not every negotiation will occur with another party with whom you have, or desire, a long-term relationship. Nevertheless, the idea is still important. Think of long-term relationships are those with individuals or organizations we value and, hence, are inclined to work hard to maintain. The stronger the working relationship, the greater the level of trust likely to permeate its character. For example, consider relationships among sports agents and owners of various teams. While professional affiliations require each to adopt adversarial roles, outside of those roles, many of these individuals maintain cordial, sometimes friendly relations with one another. Understand the differences between personal and business relationships, while acknowledging that the healthier the personal or working relationship, the more likely professional contacts are to be more positive and mutually satisfying, even in the midst of protracted negotiations.

## 2. Focus on Interests, Not Positions

There is an important difference between the positions each party adopts and the interests that underscore and mold those positions. In this context, *interests* means the fundamental motivations that frame each party's positions. As Fisher and Ury note, "Interests define the problem." It is not the position taken by each party that shapes the negotiation nearly as much as it is the interests that are the source of fear, needs, and desires. Recall that in Figure 7.1 the position of the contractor is to play hardball, hoping to get the company to do a job for something less than $1,650,000. And, although the contractor does not know this, the company will not even consider the job for less than $1,450,000. These are opposing positions. However, they do not tell us anything about the interests driving the positions. For example, rather than focusing on the contractor's desire to get the job done for somewhere between $1,250,000 and $1,450,000, the company's negotiators need to examine the motivation behind this position (i.e., the contractor's interests). Likewise, what are the company's major interests shaping its negotiating position. Interests, rather than positions, form the heart of any negotiation.

Why look for underlying interests as opposed to focusing on the positions that are on the table? Certainly, it is far easier to negotiate with another party from the point of your position versus theirs. However, there are compelling reasons why focusing on interests rather than positions offer an important leg-up in successful negotiations. First, unlike positions, for every interest there are usually several alternatives that can satisfy it. The major interest of the company in Figure 7.1 is to ensure it will be in business for many years. With this awareness, company negotiators can look for solutions other than squeezing every drop of profit out of the contractor. For example, they could enter into a long-term relationship with the contractor, in which the company forgoes some profit on this job while locking the contractor into a sole-source agreement for the next three years. The contractor would then receive the additional profit from the job by paying less than the company desires, but ensure long-term work (its interest).

Another reason for focusing on interests is that negotiating from positions often leads to roadblocks as each party tries to find their opponent's cut-off position while concealing their own. We consume valuable time and resources in posturing our various positions while hiding as long as possible our true intentions. In focusing on interests, on the other hand, we adopt a partnering mentality that acknowledges the legitimacy of both sides' interests and seeks solutions that will be mutually satisfying. Some important points about interests include:

**Identifying interests: Ask "Why?" and "Why Not?"** Put yourself in the other party's shoes. For each position they take, ask yourself, "Why?" What is the underlying interest served by adopting that position? Likewise, when confronted with the other side's positions, it is usually helpful to dissect them, asking "Why not?" for each potential alternative. Why are they adopting the attitudes they have chosen? Of course, the easiest method for identifying interests is by asking the other party, in as direct and non-threatening a manner as possible, what their major concerns and interests are. When one party is willing to share their interests in advance with the other party, it is likely that a mutually agreeable set of alternatives will be generated.

**The most powerful interests are basic human needs.** Remember that underlying much of the initial bargaining and negotiation posturing is a simple tenet: human needs define interests. Needs, as defined by Maslow, Alderfer, [2,3] and others, include issues like recognition, safety and security, a sense of belonging and acceptance, and control over one's life. Do these issues define the methods used by many negotiators? Absolutely! Consider that for many negotiators, assessing how well they did in a particular negotiation is typically framed as a win-lose proposition. Does the contractor want the extra $50,000 he can squeeze out of the company? Certainly in terms of economic self-interest the firm may need the money but other needs go deeper than that. It may be that the contractor defines himself in terms of his ability to be treated as an equal partner with other, larger firms. Therefore, in deciding to play hardball over the extra $50,000, the company may be completely misunderstanding the contractor's need to be treated with respect. The company sees this as a money issue while the contractor views it as an equity issue. Refusing to budge on the extra $50,000 may fuel his feelings of inferiority and cause entrenchment to an equally intransigent position, guaranteeing long and potentially fruitless negotiations.

**Acknowledge their interests as part of the problem.** Do not treat others' self-interests as peripheral to the issue at hand. Rather, be willing to address them head-on in such a manner that the other party feels that you are truly making an effort to be even-handed in acknowledging contrasting views. For example, it may be entirely appropriate for a project manager to sit down with a client and say, "As I understand it, your interests are primarily to get this project delivered to your site by the end of next month in order to make your major milestone. Do I understand your interests correctly? Is there anything else I need to be aware of?" In framing questions along these lines, you give the other party the opportunity to: (1) correct faulty interpretations, (2) share additional important interests, and (3) understand that you are trying to include their vital interests into any deal worked out. You will often be amazed at how quickly and positively another party will respond to your candor, particularly if you are willing to share some of your interests with them.

## 3. Invent Options for Mutual Gain

In classes on negotiation skills, one of the questions frequently asked is, "What prevents us from looking for win-win outcomes?" Typically, there are some basic responses that emerge which closely mirror those uncovered by Fisher and Ury [4]. They include:

**Premature judgment.** We quickly arrive at conclusions about the other side and anything they say usually serves to solidify our impression. Further, rather than seek to broaden our options early in the negotiation, we typically go the other direction and put limits on how much we are willing to "give up," how far we are willing to go. Every premature judgment we make limits our freedom of action and puts us deeper into an adversarial, Winners-Losers exchange.

**Searching for the "best" answer.** A common error made by unskilled negotiators is to assume that buried underneath the rhetoric and posturing is one "best" answer. In reality, most negotiations, particularly if they are to result in win-win outcomes, require us to broaden our search, not limit and focus it. Remember, most of us define the "best" answer to mean the best for me, not the other party. We prefer to think in absolute terms rather than recognizing that all problems lend themselves to multiple solutions. Indeed, it is through those multiple solutions that we are most likely to attain one that is mutually satisfying.

**The assumption of the fixed pie.** In concert with the errors generated by searching for the best answer is the assumption that there is a fixed set of alternatives available. Hence, we lock into a "I win, you lose" scenario that guarantees hardball negotiating in which no ground is given nor asked.

**Thinking that "solving their problem is their problem."** Negotiation breeds egocentrism. The greater the belief that negotiation consists of simply taking care of yourself, the greater the likelihood you will be unwilling to engage in any win-win solution. Why should you? The attitude is one of pure self-absorption. At the same time, you have little interest in acknowledging whether or not the other party has any legitimacy in their position. Ultimately, it is entirely up to them to get what they can from the negotiation, just as you are seeking to get everything you can.

If these are common problems that prevent win-win outcomes, what can be done to improve the negotiation process? There are some important guidelines we can use to strengthen the relationship between the two parties and improve the likelihood of positive outcomes. Options to consider when searching for win-win alternatives include:

- Use positive and inclusive brainstorming.
- Broaden your options.
- Identify shared interests.

The use of positive and inclusive brainstorming implies that once a negotiation process begins, during its earliest phase, we seek to include the other party in a problem-solving session to identify alternative outcomes. This approach is a far cry from the typical tactic of huddling amongst ourselves to plot negotiation strategies to use against the other team. In involving the other party in a brainstorming session, seek to convince them that you perceive the problem as a mutually solvable one requiring input and creativity from both parties. Inviting the other party to a brainstorming session of this type has a powerfully disarming effect on their initial defensiveness. It demonstrates that you are interested not in beating them, but in solving the problem. Further, it reinforces the necessity of separating the people from the problem. In this way, both parties work in cooperation to find a mutually satisfactory solution that also serves to strengthen their personal relationship.

The concept of broadening options is a direct offshoot of the notion of brainstorming. One principle reason for our inability to develop win-win outcomes is due to our natural tendency to narrow the scope of possible outcomes, usually in terms of our winning and the other party losing. Broadening options requires us to be open to alternative positions and can be a natural result of focusing on interests rather than positions. The more the other party's interests are understood and the more willing you are to dissect yours, the greater the probability that together, you can create a range of options broader than those you were initially tempted to lock yourselves into.

A third technique for improving chances for win-win outcomes is to identify shared interests. A common negotiating approach of experienced bargainers is to table the larger items to a later point in the negotiation, focusing instead on minor or peripheral issues that are more easily solved. After working together, identifying shared interests and gaining some confidence from working in a collaborative way, it is possible to reintroduce the major points. By this time both sides have begun to develop a working rhythm and a level of harmony, making it easier to look for shared interests within these larger issues.

## 4. Insist on Using Objective Criteria

Fisher and Ury [4] noted that one of the best methods for ensuring that a negotiation proceeds along substantive lines is to frame the discussion around objective criteria. Don't get bogged down in arguing perceptions or subjective evaluations. A project manager, for example, recently almost had his project scuttled because of protracted negotiations with a client over delivering an "acceptable" working prototype. The project manager had a far different interpretation of the word "acceptable" than did the client. The project manager assumed acceptable included normal bugs and teething problems while the client used the word to imply error-free. In their desire to pin the onus of responsibility on the other, neither would back away from their interpretation of the nebulous term "acceptable."

Objective data and other measurable criteria often form the best basis for accurate negotiations. When firms or individuals argue costs, prices, hours of available work, etc., they are using established standards and concepts both parties can understand with a minimum of interpretation error. The more nebulous the terms used or the more subjective the language, the greater the potential to be arguing at cross-purposes.

**Develop fair standards and procedures.** Whatever standards are used as the basis of the negotiation need to be clearly spelled out and put in terms equally meaningful to both parties. This is particularly relevant in cross-cultural negotiations where language and cultural differences often attach different meaning to common English terms or American concepts.

Several American construction firms, including Bechtel Corporation, for example, recently lodged a protest against a number of Japanese firms for collusion in dividing up biddable contracts—bid rigging—prior to a major airport project in Tokyo Bay. The Japanese companies argued they were fulfilling the terms of recent free-competition agreements by allowing Bechtel to submit a bid. Further, in Japanese society, there is nothing inherently illegal or unethical about engaging in this form of bid rigging. Clearly, both parties had very different interpretations of fair and clear bidding practices.

Fair standards and procedures require that both parties come together and negotiate from the same basic understanding of the terms, concepts, common practices, and liabilities. In project management, this is particularly relevant because construction contracting requires a universally understood set of terms and standards. When the two parties are engaged in negotiating from the point of appropriate standards, it eliminates the source of many potential misunderstandings or misinterpretations.

**Don't buy the "It's company policy" line.** Many times in negotiations opponents fall back on the "Sorry, but it's company policy" line. What these people are attempting to do is create a fall guy that lets them off the hook while attempting to win points at your expense. This appeal is often false or overblown. Your best defense against the use of "It's company policy" is to restate, as reasonably as possible, the central points to your argument. Typically, those who resort to this move are tacitly acknowledging they cannot hope to match you in a straight exchange of objective information so they are hoping to sidetrack you with a delaying move. In essence, this argument can be restated as "Don't waste my time with valid arguments. I'd like to help you but I can't."

In combating the company policy approach, your best weapon is a complete understanding of the options available. If your opponent is the only source for a resource you need, they have a strong lever to use against you. The more options at your disposal, however, the greater your ability to skirt the "company policy" line. Consider a supply company that refused to negotiate with contractors for lower prices on bulk shipments of building materials, arguing that it was contrary to company policy to even consider offering price breaks. A local contractor did some checking and discovered other sources of the material within easy driving distance and casually dropped a competitor's name at a price negotiation meeting. That same afternoon the contractor received a telephone call from the president of the supply company promising to set up a special pricing arrangement.

## Dealing With Problem Negotiators

One question frequently asked is what to do when the other party is not playing by the same set of "principled" rules you are using. In other words, how do we deal with the dirty tricks and problems from negotiators for the other side? The goal here is not to teach a set of negotiation ploys and gimmicks the reader can use in a manipulative way but rather to make the reader aware of these tricks, how to recognize their use, and how to counter them, trying to bring the other party up to your level rather than sinking to theirs.

There are a number of dirty tricks or examples of negotiation hardball. Not all of these examples offer the same degree of nastiness. Some, in fact, are simply legitimate, if hard-nosed, negotiation tactics. That does not make them any easier to deal with but it should not suggest that your opponent is somehow unprincipled. Let us examine some classic negotiation ploys and what appropriate responses to them might be:

**Extreme demands.** Many people adopt the philosophy that to get what they want, they need to first aim for the stars. Then, in backing away from these initial, seemingly ridiculous positions, they believe they are more likely to get what they really wanted in the first place. This tactic, while common, can be risky if the initial extreme demand is so off-putting to the other party that they no longer believe a negotiated solution is possible. Negotiators who use this tactic will typically seek to justify it, even with specious reasoning, rather than driving an arbitrary stake in the ground.

In responding to extreme demands, it is important not to attack the demand itself; remember, attack the problem, not the position. A highly effective technique for dealing with extreme demands is to first ask the other party to fully justify their reasoning for adopting this position. Try and uncover the logic that underlies their demand. One of two things usually happens at this point. Either the other party cannot justify the demand beyond the fact that it is extreme and they are hoping for the best or, in explaining their reasoning, you will be able to uncover and expose some error in calculation or judgment that they have committed. Contrast the following exchanges in terms of which is likelier to lead to a successful win-win settlement:

**First Approach**

*Contractor:* "I will need a minimum of two million dollars in order to do that job effectively."

*Company:* "That's ridiculous! I don't know where you pulled that number from but it's way out of line. There's no way we'd go half that far!"

**Second Approach**

*Contractor:* "I will need a minimum of two million dollars in order to do that job effectively."

*Company:* "As I understand it, pouring the footings and foundation on a square footage basis works out to about $725,000. Could you show me your figures so I can see how you came up with the figure of two million?"

In the second scenario, the company negotiator has done the homework and is trying to work with the contractor in a collaborative manner. While not giving in, this person has demonstrated they want to solve the problem with the contractor, not in spite of the contractor, setting the stage for future negotiations instead of solidifying opposing positions and encouraging both parties to dig in.

**Escalating demands.** A common variant of the "extreme demands ploy" is to raise the ante every time two parties are getting close to agreement. This tactic typically only works when one party perceives the other is more anxious to conclude the negotiation than they are. They reason that by stalling and raising demands they can continue to wring additional concessions from their opponent. A good example of this occurred in Paris during the negotiations to end the Vietnam War. U.S. Secretary of State Henry Kissinger and Le Duc To, the head negotiator for North Vietnam, went through several meetings in which one or the other would offer the hope of a quick settlement and then pull the offer back while raising the stakes and demands. This approach only works when one party perceives that time is their ally and the longer they draw-out the negotiations, the more concessions they are likely to get.

In dealing with escalating demands, the best defense is to avoid giving the impression that you are time-bound. Whether it is true or not, if the other side believes time is working to their advantage, they will exploit this tactic. Good negotiators counter escalating demands by allowing adequate time to negotiate while sticking to their position, despite the rising demands of the other party. Develop a negotiation protocol early in the process, engaging in mutual brainstorming sessions and setting standards for appropriate negotiation behaviors and unacceptable responses. Also, develop a good working relationship with the lead negotiator for the other side and work to head off attempts to raise the stakes throughout the process.

**Lock-in tactics.** Lock-in tactics represent your opponents adopting a very public and absolute position at the start of the negotiation. They are gambling that in putting themselves into a position from which they cannot retreat, you will be forced to back down and make concessions. A good example of a lock-in tactic is a labor negotiator promising to take nothing less than a 10 percent raise for his constituency, knowing that in making a public pledge, he creates a boundary around his ability to maneuver. Lock-in tactics are dangerous for a couple of reasons. First, they potentially create bad feelings between you and your opponent. The other side resents being placed in the role of the spoiler, particularly when you have defined the terms of the negotiation. Second, it is a high-risk strategy. A clever or intractable opponent may call your bluff. You are faced with the equally unpleasant options of caving in, which destroys your credibility, or continuing to stand firm while hoping the other side is also bluffing.

How do you respond to lock-in tactics? First, recognize the ploy and absolutely refuse to address the commitment itself. The more the lock-in is de-emphasized, either through humor or reason, the easier it is for the other side to back down with minimal loss of face. Many people, however, make it a policy to never yield to pressure, feeling that once they cave in, they encourage additional lock-in efforts. President George Bush adopted a lock-in strategy with his infamous "Read my lips" pledge regarding new taxes. Less than three years later, he was forced to accept a large tax hike and the bad press that came with backing away from his pledge. Skilled negotiators sought ways to redirect the bargaining process away from the pledge itself. During the actual negotiations, little was mentioned about the lock-in pledge to give the President maximum room to maneuver. In this case, however, he played directly into the hands of his political opponents who, while making the actual decision easier, crowed publicly about it afterward.

**Good cop/bad cop.** Another well-known gambit is to use a negotiating team in which one member acts belligerent, bellicose, and whose role is to be confrontational. As part of this, he will also set high demands and posture as though unwilling to consider alternatives. The partner adopts the mien of the soul of reasonableness, sometimes even publicly chastising his partner before turning apologetically back to the other negotiating party. The good cop's job is to reason with the other side, offering some moderate concession as opposed to the extreme demand, and expect the other party to be so appreciative of his candor, they will accept the marginally more reasonable offer. In effect, good cop/bad cop is classic manipulation, using the tactic of multiple points of pressure to influence the other side.

Good cop/bad cop, even when recognizable, is surprisingly effective. To avoid unpleasant exchanges with the bad cop, we quickly latch on and engage in dialogue with the good cop, exactly what the other party is working for. The bad cop's role is to be nothing more than an agent provocateur. He serves as a goad, pushing the opponent into conversations with his more accessible partner.

It is important to look beyond this fairly transparent trick and see the position the other party is adopting. The giveaway is to listen carefully to the good cop, who is the true spokesperson for the group. It is often the good cop who has authority to make the final deal and it should be to this person that most conversation is directed. Negotiate without emotion or giving in to the jibes of the bad cop.

**Take-it-or-leave-it.** Always lurking in the background of negotiations is the desire to close as quickly and painlessly as possible. Some opponents prefer to play their own game of hardball which consists of offering a "drop dead" position from which they insist they will not retreat. The benefits and drawbacks are obvious— big wins or big failures. The risks are concomitantly large. When you draw a line in the sand, you are entering into a game in which you gamble the other party needs the deal more than you. In some situations, particularly if you have done your homework, you may be correct. For example, you may discover the other side is in financial straits, forcing them to offer major concessions. On the other hand, take-it-or-leave-it is not negotiation per se. It does not allow for problem-solving or mutual win-win outcomes and, should be used rarely, and then only when you believe you hold the winning hand.

How do you deal with take-it-or-leave-it positions? First recognize that at some point all negotiations become take-it-or-leave-it. There is a final point beyond which the other party will not cross (see Figure 7.1). Your best response to a premature or unwarranted take-it-or-leave-it threat it is to downplay or ignore the implication of their stand. That is, when told to take a deal or walk away, try to rephrase or recast the position in terms of a new point from which to continue bargaining. A building contractor speaking with a supplier may say, "I understand that $1.50 is the lowest you believe you can go on a per square-inch basis for the materials. Now that we are looking at recasting our working relationship into a longer-term proposition, I'm sure you can see the advantages of both of us gaining a mutually acceptable price and delivery arrangement."

**The pressure of delaying.** Delay works only when one party is more time-bound than the other. Some individuals use delay as a tactic to increase the other side's tension and willingness to concede points. For example, refusing to return telephone calls or other contacts can make the other party pursue you. On the other hand, it is a fairly transparent tactic and can backfire, particularly if your opponent has other options available.

It is also important to distinguish between delay and the use of periodic "time outs." There is nothing wrong with using time-out in a negotiation. For example, new proposals or surprises offered at a negotiating session should always be followed by the other side taking time out to fully explore and consider them. Never take a deal that has just been placed on the table. Walk away and think about it. If the deal is genuine, it will still be there when you return, and if it is phony, the other party's pressure on you to make a quick decision is an obvious giveaway.

**Second bite at the apple.** Another common tactic involves the other side leaving themselves room to maneuver. Just when you think you have a deal worked out, your opponent will say, "Well, this looks good to me. I just need to get formal approval from my boss before we can officially close it." Guess what? Nine times out of ten this is a trick to walk away from the table only to return later with modified terms. Your opponent may couch the changes apologetically, saying "I was ready to go for it but my boss just had a couple of minor concerns." The second bite of the apple allows the other side to make maximum use of time and ambiguous lines of authority to work out a better deal. After all, if only you are in a position to make concessions, only you will make concessions.

The best method for dealing with the second bite at the apple is to set some ground rules prior to the negotiation. First, make sure the person sitting across the table from you has the authority to negotiate the deal. Ask them directly, "Who has final decision authority?" This puts them in the position of either acknowledging that they have it or admitting that someone else will have to make the decision. In the latter case, you may request future meetings include this decision-maker to save time in transmitting positions. Under no circumstances should you allow yourself to commit to an agreement that the other side will not commit to at the same time. If this situation occurs, make it clear you are not bound by the agreement should it be changed. Rather, when—or if—they come back with changes, these will form the basis of the next round of negotiations.

**Deliberate deception and phony facts.** Veteran negotiators often will admit they enjoy negotiating with brazen liars. This is because some of their exaggerations and stated positions are so outrageous they are easily countered. The trick is to do your homework prior to the negotiation. For example, in negotiating with a car salesman who is making false claims about the cost of a new automobile, get a copy of the actual cost from *Consumer Reports.* Armed with this information, you are in a better position to catch the other party in some of their more obvious deceptions.

**Remember some important guidelines for dealing with deceptive negotiators.** First, there is a difference between outright fraud and simply withholding information. No good negotiator is likely to lay all their cards on the table up front. They want to see just how much you understand about the issue at hand. A good example happened recently while I was traveling in Europe. In purchasing a train ticket, the counterman held a fistful of bills and proceeded to count some out and drop them on the counter. He then paused and waited for a response. Remaining there and waiting for him to hand over all the change avoided accusing him of fraud—or was he stealing? Had I picked up the change at that point, he would have pocketed the balance of the change that he was still holding. He was simply gauging my response to his opening position. The principle is the same in business negotiations, it is your responsibility to recognize the difference between what your opponent chooses to tell you and the rest of the story.

Your second defense in dealing with deceptive negotiators is equally simple—do your homework. It is amazing the number of novice negotiators who walk into their first bargaining sessions with only a cursory understanding of their own positions, let alone any knowledge of the other party. The difference between a good chess player and an exceptional chess player is the latter is always anticipating several moves ahead. They know the game intimately and they understand the appropriate responses for most situations and moves. In doing your homework, remember to look beyond your opponent's positions and consider their interests. What is driving their behavior? The more you learn about the other side, the better your chances of correctly anticipating and responding to their moves.

Finally, Fisher and Ury [4] make an important point about trust. Essentially, they argue that unless you have compelling reasons to trust the other party, do not. That is not to suggest that you call them liar. Instead you are attempting to separate the people from the problem. Your doubts about another party are not intended as a personal attack, nor should you allow the other side to frame them this way. "Don't you trust me? I thought we had a good relationship here." Trust is a separate issue. You are working to make the best arrangement you can, just as you should reasonably assume that the other individual is working along similar lines. The more you make clear your willingness and intent to verify all factual information, particularly early in the negotiation, the greater the incentive for your opponent to provide you with legitimate information.

**Personal attacks.** Some extremely successful negotiators have a very limited set of tactics for negotiation. Essentially, they operate under the belief the faster they can get the other party angry and emotional, the greater the chance for securing some major concession, because the other party is so anxious to end the negotiation they walk away quickly, getting a mediocre deal with minimal effort. The use of personal attacks is blatant psychological manipulation and one of the dirtier negotiating tricks. Most of us are uncomfortable with negotiations. These bullies understand this and seek to capitalize on our hesitancy by pouring gasoline on the fire. Their reasoning is simple. The more unpleasant they make the process, the sooner you will capitulate and grant them the major points.

The tactic of personal attack is very shortsighted. No one engaging in mind games with a bully is anxious to do so again. Consequently, most abusive negotiators employ this tactic in situations involving one-shot deals, where they can walk away secure in the knowledge they have won and are unlikely to ever see the other party again. There are two responses to personal attacks. The first is to recognize the tactic and refuse to allow yourself to be drawn into it. The longer you stay cool in the face of this sort of sniping, the sooner the other party will acknowledge its futility and call it off. The second option for handling abuse is to call your opponent on his or her behavior as it occurs. A writer on office politics once noted, "Leave no shot unanswered" [5]. This is not to suggest you return insult or innuendo in kind, but rather that you tell the other person you know what game he is playing and refuse to go along with it.

### What can we do in dealing with problem negotiators?
Remember, all of these tactics are designed to throw you off your game. In each case, your opponent is using a method that he believes will secure him some advantage. It is not personal. Nevertheless, you do have some alternatives when these attacks occur. In addition to those mentioned, there are some general rules and guidelines that can make dealing with problem negotiators easier for everyone.

**Don't attack their position, look behind it.** Recognize the basic motivations driving your opponent. Their behavior is simply a physical manifestation of the deeper issues that underscore their negotiating position and behavior. Is ego driving them? A desire to succeed and look good for the boss? Is it a personal vendetta, or is their behavior the result of their own inexperience? In framing your response, avoid getting into a series of escalating exchanges with the other party. No one wins in a free-for-all, and from a negotiation standpoint, it is counterproductive. Directly assaulting their position only causes the other party to dig their heels in. Rather, make it clear you are seeking a mutually satisfying alternative, understanding their interests and working to address them.

**Recast an attack on you as an attack on the problem.** Many people cannot understand a basic law of negotiation—the person is not the position. We make a mistake when we make the person across the table from us the physical manifestation of all that we object to in the other party's position, often framing them as the bad guys because of their espousal of those views. Consider, for example, the attitudes shared by many people about defense lawyers who, many are convinced, have no morality because of their willingness to defend any felon, no matter how reprehensible. Obviously, we are imparting all of our animus regarding crime in general, the court system, the justice system, law as a profession, and so forth, on the lawyer. Fair or not, this individual becomes the scapegoat for our dissatisfaction.

Many of us do the same thing in negotiations. The other side becomes the symbol of the opposing position and, as such, we are tempted to develop supporting negative stereotypes about them as individuals. It is important to understand that we must look behind the individual to the position and to the underlying issues. That is, to seek ways to deflect the attack toward a mutually acceptable problem. When faced with personal attacks, rather than respond defensively, recast the attack onto the problem. "When you say that you do not like my use of your subordinates on the project, I'm hearing your concern that organizational resources be used as efficiently as possible. I want you to know that I share this concern. Could you give me some of your thoughts on how best to move the project through the system while using your people efficiently?"

**Understand the uses and advantages of silence.** Silence makes most people uncomfortable. In certain situations (e.g., riding in an elevator, waiting for a bus) we often find ourselves engaging in the most mundane or superficial conversations with strangers in an effort to avoid the pain of silence. In fact, silence is a wonderful tool to negotiate better deals. When engaged in negotiations with another party, don't feel compelled to be the one to break the silence. Wait for the other party to initiate discussions. The result is often that you are now in the position of responding to their opening gambits or offers rather than having the onus of initiation placed on you. Silence is particularly useful when the other party is attempting to use personal attacks or extreme demands as a negotiating tactic. Rather than respond, particularly when you are not sure what to say, keep silent. Pretty quickly, someone on the other side will put their own interpretation on your reticence—perhaps that you are offended, angry, or simply intractable, and adjust their position accordingly.

A classic example of this tactic is a story about President Lyndon Johnson who, when meeting Soviet Premier Alexi Kosygin for the first time, proceeded to stare at him silently for well over a half hour until Kosygin was the first to break eye contact. Obviously, for most of us, silence does not have to constitute a battle of wills or a machismo display, nor is it always the best approach to take in principled negotiation. Nevertheless, many of us have discovered we can learn a great deal more and concede a great deal less when we listen rather than talk.

## Summary

Negotiation is a process that few of us relish. Project managers are no different. While their job often consists of a series of negotiations, with clients, upper management, the project team, and other stakeholder groups, many have never thought to systematically develop a strategy for these negotiation processes. Further, once placed in the bargaining position, they refuse to acknowledge all the options available, perhaps preferring to follow tried-and-true methods (regardless of the fact that they may not be well-tried or even true).

Negotiation, in its basic sense, is a form of influence that is conducted around a formal goal. As it relates to influence and, ultimately, a project manager's political acumen, it is important to learn to better employ these techniques. The first step is an honest assessment of current deficiencies regarding negotiating. How would we honestly rate ourselves in this activity? Once we have an image in our minds of our proficiency or lack thereof, the second step is to begin examining precisely what our weak points are. Do we too quickly personalize a negotiation? Do we automatically assume all negotiations are win-lose? Do we look for underlying interests, or are we content to simply deal with positions? Finally, do we do our homework or do we approach every negotiation as a real-time survival of the fittest? The answers to these questions will go a long way toward improving our negotiation abilities.

## chapter 8

# Conflict and Project Management

*Madness is the exception in individuals but the rule in groups.*
Nietzsche

**P**roject managers face conflict as part of their daily life from a number of sources, internal and external, and in dealing with other project stakeholders [1, 2, 3]. One study estimated that the average manager spends over 20 percent of his or her time dealing with conflict [4]. Project managers would likely suggest that the 20 percent figure understates the case! Conflict is often an offshoot of power struggles and political dynamics with an organization. Because so much of a project manager's time is taken up with active conflict and its aftermath, it is important to examine this process within the project management context.

In the past, much has been written about the sources of conflict within the project management context. Little, however, is known or understood about the actual dynamics of the conflict process itself. That is, once a conflict occurs, what are some of the common responses and actions that are fairly predictable? This chapter explores the process of conflict, examines the various sources of conflict for project teams and managers, develops a model of conflict behavior, and fosters an understanding of some of the most common methods for de-escalating conflict. Many conflicts develop out of a basic lack of or unwillingness to understand another party's position. And once a conflict does occur, either within or outside the project team, project managers who are aware of the various action alternatives they can employ have a real opportunity to not only defuse conflict but also to learn valuable lessons from the episode. Understanding these issues well will improve project managers' use of power, make them better at their job, reduce stress, and enhance the team environment.

## What is Conflict?

One of the best definitions of conflict suggests it is the process that begins when one perceives that one or more others have frustrated or are about to frustrate a major concern of theirs [5, 6]. There are two important elements in this definition. First, it suggests that conflict is not a "state" per se, but a process. As such, it contains a very important dynamic aspect: conflicts evolve [2]. Further, the one-time causes of a conflict may change over time; that is, the reasons why a conflict started between two individuals or groups may no longer be valid. However, because the conflict state is dynamic and evolving, once a conflict has occurred, the reasons behind it may no longer matter.

Second, conflict is perceptual in nature. It does not ultimately matter whether or not one party has truly frustrated another party. The key is that one party perceives that state or event to have occurred. That perception is enough because, for the first party, perception of frustration defines their reality.

## Sources of Conflict

There are an enormous number of potential sources for conflict. Some of the most common include competition for scarce resources, violations of group or organizational norms, disagreements over goals or the means to achieve those goals, personal slights and threats to job security, long-held biases and prejudices, and so forth. Many of the sources of conflict arise from the positions of managers or the nature of the work they do. Another equally compelling set of causes also stem from the individuals themselves; that is, their own psychological processes contribute to the level and amount of conflict within an organization. One useful method of looking at the causes of conflict is to separate the organizational and interpersonal causes of conflict.

## Organizational Sources of Conflict

Some of the most common organizational causes of conflict include:

- Reward systems
- Scarce resources
- Uncertainty over lines of authority
- Differentiation.

Reward systems are often a source of conflict because, in some organizations, there are in place competitive reward systems that pit one group or functional department against another. When functional managers, for example, are evaluated on the performance of their subordinates, they are loath to allow their best workers to become involved in project work for any length of time. The organization may have unwittingly created a situation where functional managers perceive that either the project teams or the departments, but not both, will be rewarded for superior performance. In such cases, they will naturally retain their best people for functional duties and offer less-desirable subordinates for project team work. The project managers, on the other hand, will also perceive a competition between their projects and the functional departments and develop a strong sense of animosity toward functional managers who they perceive, with some justification, are putting their interests above the organization.

By its very nature, a project generates significant differences of opinion in how scarce resources, particularly personnel and money, are used. Project managers face an on-going battle with functional managers to get the resources needed for a successful project. This easily leads to confrontation not only between project managers and department heads, but also between the functional managers who know one or more of them will lose resources.

Uncertainty over lines of authority asks the tongue-in-cheek question, "Who's in charge around here?" In the project environment, it is easy to see how this problem can be exacerbated due to the ambiguity that exists in terms of formal channels of authority. Project managers and their teams sit "outside" the formal organizational hierarchy in many organizations. As a result, they find themselves in a uniquely fragile position of having a great deal of autonomy but also responsibility to the functional department heads who provide the personnel for the team. When a project team member from R&D, for example, is given orders by a functional manager that subsume or directly contradict directives from the project manager, the team member is placed in the dilemma of finding, if possible, a middle ground between two authority figures. In many cases, project managers do not have the authority to prepare performance evaluations of team members, that control is kept within the functional department. In such situations, the team member from R&D, facing role conflict brought on by this uncertainty over lines of authority, will most likely do the expedient thing and obey functional managers because of their "power of the performance appraisal."

The final source of organizational conflict, differentiation, suggests that as individuals join an organization within some functional specialty, they begin to adopt the attitudes and outlook of that functional group. For example, when asked for an opinion of marketing, a member of the finance department might reply, "All they ever do is travel around and spend money. They're a bunch of cowboys who would give away the store if they had to." Marketing's response would follow along the lines of, "Finance people are just a group of bean-counters who don't understand that the company is only as successful as it can sell its products. They're so hung up on their margins, they don't know what goes on in the real world." Now the important point in each of these views is that, within their narrow frames of reference, they are both essentially correct. Marketing is interested primarily in making sales and finance is devoted to maintaining high margins. These opinions, however, are by no means completely true. Instead they reflect the underlying attitudes and prejudices of members of both functional departments. The more profound the differentiation within an organization, the greater the likelihood of individuals and groups dividing up into "us" versus "them" encampments, which continue to promote and provoke conflict.

## Interpersonal Causes of Conflict

In addition to these organizational causes of conflict, consider also some of the salient interpersonal causes. While by no means a comprehensive list, among these interpersonal sources of conflict are:

- Faulty attributions
- Faulty communication
- Grudges and prejudices.

Faulty attributions refers to misconceptions of the reasons behind another's behavior. When people perceive their interests have been thwarted by another individual or group, they typically try to determine why the other party acted as they did. In making attributions about another's actions, we try to determine if their motives are based on personal malevolence, hidden agendas, and so forth. Often, groups and individuals will attribute motives to other's actions that are personally most convenient. When one member of a project team, for example, has his or her wishes frustrated, it is common to perceive the motives behind the other party's actions in terms of the most convenient causes. In other words, rather than acknowledge that reasonable people may differ in their opinions, the frustrated person may assume the other is provoking a conflict for personal reasons, "He just doesn't like me." This attribution is convenient for an obvious and psychologically "safe" reason. If we assume the other person disagrees with us for valid reasons, it implies a flaw in our position. Many individuals do not have the ego-strength to acknowledge and accept objective disagreement, preferring to couch their frustration in personal terms.

A very common, interpersonal cause of conflict stems from faulty communication. This implies the potential for two mistakes: (1) communicating in ambiguous ways which leads to different interpretations, resulting in conflict, and (2) unintentionally communicating in ways that annoy or anger other parties. Lack of clarity sends out mixed signals: some will understand the message the sender intended to communicate, others will interpret it differently. Consequently, a project manager may be surprised and annoyed by a subordinate's work while the subordinate may genuinely think he or she is adhering to the project manager's desires. Likewise, project managers often engage in criticism hoping to correct and improve a project team members' performance. Unfortunately, what the project manager may consider to be harmless, constructive criticism may come across as a destructive, unfair critique if the information is not communicated accurately and effectively.

Interpersonal conflict refers to the personal grudges and prejudices that each of us brings to any work situation. These attitudes arise as the result of long-term experiences or lessons taught at some point in the past. Often unconsciously held, we may be unaware we nurture these attitudes and may feel a genuine sense of affront when we are challenged or accused of holding biases. Nevertheless, these grudges or prejudices, whether they are held against another race, sex, or functional department, have a seriously debilitating effect on our ability to work with others in a purposeful team and can ruin any chance of project team cohesion and subsequent project performance.

## Steps in the Conflict Process

Regardless of the triggering cause, once conflicts, either intra- or intergroup, have begun, they tend to follow a rather well-defined pattern. It is useful for project managers to be aware of this pattern because it serves as a template to recognize various conflict dynamics. If the nature of the conflict process is understood as it progresses, one is in a better position to search for methods to defuse and minimize the conflict or channel its energies into more constructive pastimes. In this section, we examine the stages in the conflict process and offer some suggestions for project managers on how to most effectively deal with the conflict dynamics that often emerge.

Typically, there are five recognizable stages in the conflict process:

- Frustration
- Conceptualization
- Orientation
- Interaction
- Outcome.

### Frustration

The first stage of any conflict process is triggered by an event that sets one or more people at odds. As suggested in the original definition of conflict, this event is referred to as "perceived frustration." Frustration comes in many forms and approaches. Earlier, we identified several sources of frustration, and classified them into two categories: organizational and interpersonal. The important point to remember is that frustrations occur in everyone's life on a daily basis. Therefore, there must be some reason why we respond to certain frustrations in a confrontational manner but not to others. Often, this choice is predicated on our perception of how important the issue is to us. Under normal circumstances, a traffic jam would be a source of frustration, but we would rarely deem it serious enough to actively confront the city administration over the issue. On the other hand, in situations that involve slights to status, promotion possibilities, or public image, we tend to react to frustrations more directly. It is these situations, where we attach a level of importance to the frustrated goal, when we are most likely to respond in an aggressive and competitive manner.

## Conceptualization

Conceptualization means defining the issues underlying the source of conflict. Analyze why a conflict is occurring between ourselves and our team or with someone else, and an interesting psychological process begins to occur. We see the conflict through the lens of egocentricity. Egocentricity refers to the predilection of most people to define issues solely in terms of their own concerns. When confronted with a situation in which we feel frustrated by another individual, we respond in a way that does not recognize the other party's perspective. That is, we perceive the other person is thwarting us, without considering their point of view or why they are acting in a particular way.

The clear alternative to analyzing frustration in terms of egocentricity is to develop insight into the other party's concerns. Remember, never judge another person unless you have walked a mile in their shoes. Unless another person's motives, intent, and past experiences are understood, we cannot objectively address the nature of the conflict. Rather, we will continue to be inclined to respond with an egocentric approach that only further solidifies the lines that separate the rival parties' positions. Attempting to gain this insight into the underlying issues involves refusing to capitulate to the initial sense of frustration with another party and search for reasons why that person or group is operating the way they are.

It is this search for the answer to "why" that will defuse many conflicts before they escalate. It requires the project manager or team member to be able to forego the appeals of egocentricity and to try and analyze the problem from the other party's perspective. Depending upon the nature and degree of conflict, this rational objectivity can be very difficult, but well worth the effort. If we halt conflicts at this stage, many of the problems that would continually plague the project team throughout the project can be avoided.

## Orientation

Orientation is the outlook we begin to adopt as a conflict episode continues to escalate. Thomas [5] and Ruble and Thomas [7] argue that conflict orientation generally involves operating along two separate dimensions of concern: (1) the degree to which one party seeks to satisfy their own concerns, and (2) the degree to which a party seeks to satisfy the other person's concerns. Figure 8.1 shows Ruble and Thomas' [7] conceptualization of this two-dimensional model of conflict orientation. They argue we make implicit trade-offs in our willingness to seek our gains versus our willingness to satisfy the other party to the conflict. They further posit that the underlying motive driving these two dimensions is our desire to be assertive and gain maximum advantage while being cooperative with the other party in order to maintain satisfactory relationships [8].

Within this two-dimensional model of conflict orientation and behavior, Thomas suggests five distinct and recognizable types of conflict behavior are potentially possible:

- Competing
- Accommodating
- Avoiding
- Compromising, and
- Collaborating.

The decision of which type of behavior to engage in resides solely with the party who is conceptualizing the nature and reasons for the conflict. Figure 8.2 shows each of the five conflict-handling styles.

Competing behavior is basically assertive and uncooperative. Someone adopting a competing style has no regard for satisfying the other party's concerns, viewing conflict as a win-lose proposition in which they have resolved not to lose. Competing behavior is often used by insecure or power-hungry people who will use every technique and trick to get their way. It is often ironic to find that individuals who are high on the competing dimension have great difficulty in operating under any other style, no matter what the nature of the conflict. For example, highly competitive people take issues of resource allocation and the results of a game of gin rummy with the same degree of intensity. They cannot distinguish between "important" conflicts and "unimportant" conflicts; indeed, the very

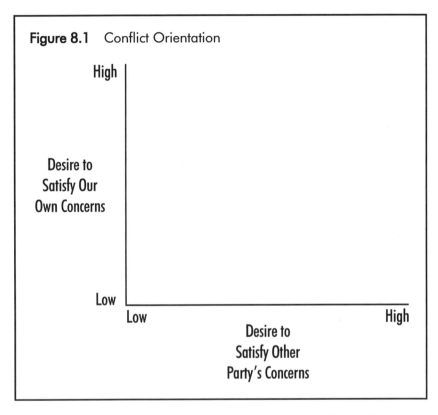

**Figure 8.1** Conflict Orientation

existence of a concept such as an "unimportant" conflict is alien to their way of thinking.

At the opposite extreme from competing behavior is the accommodating style. As Figure 8.2 shows, accommodators enter conflict from the perspective of seeking to first satisfy the other party's concerns. Accommodators foster nonassertive and cooperative styles, usually in an effort to be true "team players." They are quick to look for ways to defuse a situation or to allow the other party to win. The accommodating style can be useful when the issue of concern is seen as more important for the other side than for the accommodator. It may serve as an important goodwill gesture or a basis for "storing up" favors the manager may need at a later point. If overused, however, the accommodating style tends to create passivity in a project manager, a state which can deprive subordinates or peers of useful viewpoints and contributions.

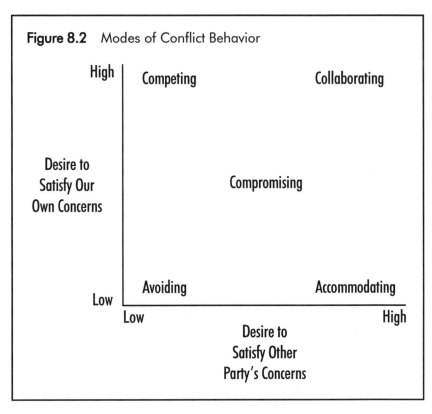

**Figure 8.2** Modes of Conflict Behavior

The avoiding style is one that is both unassertive and uncooperative. Individuals who rely on the avoiding style manifest no desire to either satisfy their concerns or the concerns of the other party to the conflict. Avoiding tends to be an effective method for sidestepping a conflict that one party does not seek. It is the style of organizational diplomats and politicians who perceive they can accomplish more if they operate behind the scenes rather than in the open, in conflict with another party.

Compromising behavior falls somewhere between assertive and cooperative behavior. It is a desire by one party to satisfy some of their concerns and a willingness to give in on other points. A compromiser sees conflict as a win-lose situation and believes that in order to get something it is necessary to give up something else. A compromising style tacitly acknowledges the importance of making concessions to gain something from the conflict. As a result, while compromisers see conflict in terms of winners and losers, they generally feel that each party can win a little and lose a little.

Collaborating behavior rates high on both assertiveness and cooperativeness. Collaborators view conflict from a very different perspective than most managers in that they reject the win-lose argument most of us believe underlies conflict. Always seeking a win-win solution, to achieve such an outcome, collaborators readily work with the other party to see if it is possible to find a solution that fully satisfies both sides. This sort of joint problem solving requires a great deal of flexibility, creativity, and precise communication between the parties in conflict.

A collaborating style is usually necessary when the issue at hand is too important to be solved with a compromising approach. In situations when project leaders are seeking to make major product specification changes or determine resource allocation, they may be faced with two or more distinct alternatives. Rather than vainly attempt to satisfy these disparate viewpoints by offering a compromise that will please no one and do nothing to further the development of the project, these managers may hold a series of project team meetings to get all positions on the table where they can be addressed in a problem-solving session. The result of this meeting may be a new strategic focus for the project with new tasks and responsibilities for each team member. In this meeting, the problem underlying the conflict could not be ignored. Further, allowing one team member to dominate the others with a competing style could potentially result in an incorrect decision. The best alternative for the project manager is to find, in collaboration with the project team, a solution that offers a win-win alternative.

Because no one conflict-handling style is appropriate in every situation, insightful project managers develop flexibility in their approaches to dealing with conflicts, either their own or those of team members within the group. The benefits of a collaborative style is that, unlike competing or avoiding, a collaborative style emphasizes group relationships. Using this style offers a method for enhancing communication and creative problem solving. In doing so, a collaborating approach can bring a team in conflict closer together, rather than driving them further apart by solidifying the conflict situation.

## Interaction

Once a conflict episode escalates, a number of different exchanges begin to occur between the two parties in conflict. This exchange process is referred to as conflict interaction. While there are many actions conflicting parties can take during this process, our focus is on some of the more common dynamics of group conflict during this stage.

One common occurrence, usually early in the conflict, is reinforcement through stereotyping. When another party is frustrating a goal we value, we often respond by attributing their intransigence to convenient (and often incorrect) motives. For example, in a budgeting dispute with the project accountant, a project manager may react by saying, "What can you expect from a group of unimaginative bean-counters?" This reaction, while common, underscores the potential for reinforcing the disagreement by creating a self-serving stereotype of the other party. In this process, all opponents are selfish, willfully ignorant, or malicious because these attributions allow us to hold the high ground in the dispute.

Through stereotyping other professions, cultures, races, or the opposite sex, we create a cause for discontent without being forced to reexamine our motives as a potential contributor to the conflict. As the name of this process suggests, rather than attempting to defuse or suppress tension, the first inclination is to reinforce the conflict, making it that much more difficult to correct.

Another process likely during the interaction phase is one in which conflict begins to heighten feelings of positive identification with one's own group. There is a tendency, when we perceive a conflict with an external stakeholder, to close ranks and become more single-minded in our attitudes and dispositions. As a result of that process, it is common for groups to develop a superiority complex vis-à-vis the other group. This superiority complex feeds our inclinations to regard our position as sacrosanct and justified as opposed to the "devious" and "maliciously inclined" opponents.

On a national level, this positive identification dynamic occurs quite frequently. For instance: In the early 1980s, just prior to the Falkland War with Great Britain, Argentina was in a state of tremendous political turmoil. Crowds in Buenos Aires and other large cities continually protested the right-wing rule of the military junta that controlled the government, until Argentina invaded the

Falklands, and created an external foe. Overnight, the crowds that had been demonstrating against the government became vast throngs supporting their leaders, united in their opposition to Great Britain. This is an example of the positive identification effect that occurs in the face of external conflict.

Another dynamic likely during the action phase is exaggerating the positive nature of our group and its members, and distorting and exaggerating differences between our group and the opponent. Once we find ourselves in a conflict situation, there is pressure to conform to group norms, swallow internal differences, and deny any degree of similarity with the opposing group. This separation solidifies differences, making it harder for the groups to seek common ground. In fact, we actively avoid the potential for identifying commonalties, preferring to focus on the differences and the reasons that justify our beliefs.

## Outcome

The final stage of the conflict process is the outcome, two parties reaching an agreement, resolving the conflict. It is important to realize, however, no matter what the outcome—full agreement, or a tacit understanding—there will be residual emotions and ill will from the process. Individuals do not forgive and immediately forget conflict episodes, particularly if the issues were significant or the emotional commitment brought the conflict to a personal level. Project managers must be cognizant of the likely detritus of conflict. Playing down or smoothing over a problem when it has been "resolved" may be overly simplistic and ignores the potential for further tensions.

A final point about the outcome: Realizing the difference between short-term and long-term outcomes. Understand the truth in the phase, "Win the battle and lose the war." When a manager wins a conflict, there is a potential that the other party will remember the experience and look for retribution opportunities. This is particularly true in the case of a manager who is prone to rely solely on a competing style in dealing with conflicts. A competing approach, based on assertiveness and lack of concern for the other party, is likely to create bad feelings on the part of the other party. Whether that party wins or loses the conflict, they are likely to remember the event and seek ways to repay the other group [9].

---

**Table 8.1**   Methods for Resolving Conflict

**Avoidance**
- Non-attention
- Physical separation
- Limited interaction
- Forced interaction

**Defusion**
- Smoothing
- Compromise

**Confrontation**
- Problem-solving

---

# Methods for Resolving Conflict

A number of methods for resolving inter- and intra-group conflict are at the project manager's disposal. Before a decision is made about what approach will be employed, it is paramount for project managers to consider a number of relevant issues [10]. For example, will siding with one party to the dispute alienate the other party? Is the conflict professional or personal in nature? Does any sort of intervention have to occur or can team members resolve the issue on their own? Does the project manager have the time and inclination to mediate the dispute? All of these questions play a role in determining how to approach a conflict situation. Project managers need to learn to develop flexibility in dealing with conflict, assessing and prioritizing situations in which it is appropriate to intervene and those in which the sounder course is to adopt a neutral style.

As Table 8.1 illustrates, it is helpful to categorize possible conflict resolution methods into three fundamental philosophies: avoidance, defusion, and confrontation. Each approach has its benefits and drawbacks and, more importantly, each may be an appropriate response under certain circumstances.

## Avoidance

Avoidance techniques suggest that the project manager ignore the causes of the conflict and allow it to continue under controlled circumstances. Avoidance is a conflict-handling approach that requires the project manager to adopt a position of neutrality and passivity, while the parties to the conflict work out their differences. An example of avoidance is non-attention—the project manager simply looks the other way and allows the parties in conflict to come to their own resolution without stepping in. Mark McCormack [11], in his entertaining work *What They Still Don't Teach You At Harvard Business School*, points to a situation in which two of his vice presidents had developed an antagonism based on personal dislike, not professional reasons. He states that when conflict is of a personal and emotionally charged nature, a prudent manager will often refuse to intervene, sending signals that this sort of interaction is unacceptable, but otherwise expecting the warring parties to work out their differences.

Other types of avoidance techniques are physical separation, limited interaction, and forced interaction. These approaches are similar in requiring project managers with subordinates in conflict to find ways to keep those involved out of each other's way. When they must be together, the project team leader plays the role of referee, making sure that the conflict is kept at bay for the course of the meeting.

An alternative to limited interaction may be its exact opposite: forced interaction. In this scenario, the project manager gives two subordinates a task which requires them to work harmoniously or both will end up looking equally guilty. As a result, they are forced to lay aside their differences and cooperate for the sake of the project, for which each held joint responsibility.

In each of these techniques, rather than refraining from seeking the source of conflict, the project manager pays attention to ensuring the fallout from subordinate conflict does not impact on the project's development. This may be in vein, however, as frequent or intense conflict can force team members to expend tremendous amounts of energy on worthless pursuits. A decision to adopt an avoidance tactic in the face of subordinate conflict should be made with due consideration of the implications of allowing the conflict to continue.

## Defusion

Defusion techniques are an attempt to buy time until both parties have a chance to cool down and deal with the conflict in a more "rational" manner. As in the case of avoidance techniques, defusion approaches do not seek the underlying causes of the conflict. They are intended to address the unintended consequences once a conflict situation exists. One defusion technique is referred to as smoothing, which involves the project manager playing down group differences and emphasizing commonalties. Using this approach, a project manager might say, "Come on, people. We are all on the same side here. Let's get together to work on the project." Smoothing represents appeals to professionalism or to the group's commitment to higher goals (the organization, the project, etc.).

A second defusion technique is compromise. Compromise refers to the implicit assumption that for one party to the conflict to win on some points they must be willing to give up others. The compromise approach is classic "give and take" management, and as with smoothing, does not require the project manager to plumb the root causes of the conflict. It arbitrates the process once it is under way.

## Confrontation

The final conflict-resolution method is confrontation, best represented by problem-solving meetings. Unlike the other two sets of conflict resolution methods, confrontation requires project managers to seek and expose the causes underlying the conflict. Each source, personal, professional, or both, is identified and discussed at length, so that parties to the conflict have the opportunity to put issues out on the table where they can be addressed and resolved. Problem-solving meetings are difficult, requiring a project manager to have patience, nerves, and poise. When a manager seeks the causes of a conflict, it is akin to attempting to understand the other individuals' underlying motives and goals. Frequently, the parties involved are hesitant to open themselves up and examine basic beliefs and biases. Hence, the problem-solving process is often lengthy, accompanied by high emotions, intransigence, and obstructions from the parties concerned. Problem-solving meetings are often necessary for future project team operations, but contain an element of risk. If the meeting is not handled well, it can solidify conflict and ill will between group members, making future cooperative activities more difficult.

## Summary

In attempting to resolve conflict, each of the approaches outlined may be appropriate in different situations. A problem-solving session is not always beneficial or warranted, nor is it fair to say non-attention is always "lazy" management. Project managers must learn to understand their own preferences when it comes to handling conflict. Once a greater sense of self-awareness about our own predilections is achieved, we will be in a far better position to resolve our own conflicts constructively and deal more effectively with subordinate conflicts. The key is flexibility. It is important not to lock into any particular conflict style nor favor one resolution tactic to the exclusion of all others. Each have strengths and drawbacks that the project manager should know as part of his toolkit.

Many noted writers on project management have pointed to the inevitability of conflict in the project development process [12, 13]. Conflict comes from a variety of sources and for a myriad of reasons. It is essentially impossible for a project manager to run a team and develop a project without having to confront a number of conflicts along the way. In this chapter, we developed a framework for the organizational conflict process, examined some common causes of conflict and argued that the unique nature of project-based work makes it a natural environment in which conflicts will develop. We outlined a model of the conflict process and showed that when project managers understand the common steps, they are in a better position to defuse the conflict or use it constructively to further the project's goals. Conflict has potential to delay and even kill a project unless managers learn how to recognize its characteristics and harness the energy appropriately. Conflict is inevitable, it is not disastrous. The degree to which a conflict disrupts a project's development depends upon the project manager's willingness to learn enough about conflict to deal with it effectively.

## chapter 9

# Managerial Implications: What Do We Do?

U nderstanding the political side of organizations and the often intensely political nature of system implementation gives rise to the concomitant need to develop appropriate attitudes and strategies that help project managers operate effectively within the system. If this approach is necessary for effective project implementations, what are some steps project managers can take to become politically astute?

**Understand and acknowledge the political nature of most organizations.** In dealing with individuals suffering from a variety of illnesses, therapists and counselors of all types have long taken as their starting point the importance of the patients' acknowledgment that they have a problem. Positive results cannot be achieved in a state of continued denial. While this analogy does not hold completely true for organizational politics, the underlying point is still important: denial of the political nature of organizations does not make that phenomenon any less potent. Organizations in both the public and private sectors are inherently politicized [1]. In offering this view, we may offend those who are uncomfortable with the idea of politics and believe that through the combined efforts of all organizational actors it is possible to eradicate the political nature of companies or governmental agencies. Politics, however, are too deeply rooted within organizational operations to be treated as some aberrant form of bacteria or diseased tissue that can be excised from the organization's body.

Before managers are able to learn to use politics in a manner that is supportive of project implementation, they must first acknowledge

(1) its existence, and (2) its impact on project success. Once there is an understanding of the political nature of organizations, it is possible to develop some action steps that will aid in project implementation.

**Learn to cultivate "appropriate" political tactics.** There are appropriate and inappropriate methods for using politics. Since the purpose of all political behavior is to develop and keep power, both the politically naive and shark personalities are equally misguided and, perhaps surprisingly, equally damaging to the likelihood of project implementation success. A project manager who, either through naiveté or stubbornness, refuses to exploit the political arena is destined to be not nearly as effective in introducing the project as is a project team leader who knows how to use politics effectively. On the other hand, project managers so politicized as to appear predatory and aggressive to their colleagues are doomed to create an atmosphere of such distrust and personal animus that there is little chance for successful project adoption.

Pursuing the middle ground of political sensibility is the key to project implementation success. The process of developing and applying appropriate political tactics means using politics as it can most effectively be used as a basis for negotiation and bargaining. Politically sensible managers understand that initiating any sort of organizational disruption or change in developing a new project is bound to reshuffle the distribution of power within the organization. That effect is likely to make many departments and managers nervous as they begin to wonder how future power relationships will be rearranged. "Politically sensible" implies being politically sensitive to the concerns—real or imagined—of powerful stakeholder groups. Legitimate or not, their concerns about the new project are real and must be addressed. Appropriate political tactics and behavior include making alliances with powerful members of other stakeholder departments, networking, negotiating mutually acceptable solutions to seemingly insoluble problems, and recognizing that most organizational activities are predicated on the give-and-take of negotiation and compromise [2]. It is through these uses of political behavior that managers of project implementation efforts put themselves in the position to effectively influence the successful introduction of their systems.

146

In an article on project management and the nature of power, Lovell [3] makes a similar point, arguing that effective project managers must work to maintain constructive political alliances with powerful senior management and influential department managers. He further suggests that the persuasive skills and political acumen of a seasoned project manager will allow him or her to understand and make use of the organization's power environment, the positions of the various stakeholders, the time and means to develop and maintain alliances, and how to move around political roadblocks. Each skill requires objectivity and sensitivity from project managers in order to be successful.

**Understand and accept "WIIFM."** One of the hardest lessons for newcomers to organizations to learn is the consistently expressed and displayed primacy of departmental loyalties and self-interest over organization-wide concerns. There are many times when novice managers will feel frustrated at the unwillingness of other departments and individuals to accept new ideas or systems that are "good for them." It is vital for these managers to understand the beauty of a new project is truly in the eyes of the beholder. One may be absolutely convinced a project will be beneficial to the organization; however, convincing members of other departments of this truth is a different matter altogether.

Other departments and project stakeholders are not likely to offer their help and support of a project unless they perceive it is in their interests to do so—assuming that these departments understand the value of a project is simplistic and usually wrong. Bob Graham, a noted project management consultant, refers to the "WIIFM" in describing the reactions of stakeholder groups to new innovations. WIIFM—What's In It For Me?—is the question most often asked by individuals and departments when presented with requests for their aid. They are asking why they should support the process of implementing a new project. The worst mistake project managers can make is to assume that the stakeholders will automatically appreciate and value the project as much as they themselves do. Graham's point is that time and care must be taken to use politics effectively, to cultivate a relationship with power holders, and to make the deals needed to bring the system online. This is the essence of political sensibility: being level-headed enough to have few illusions about the difficulties one is likely to encounter in attempting to develop and implement a new project.

**Try to provide project managers with some "equal footing."** A functional line manager often views the initiation of a new project with a degree of suspicion and trepidation because of its potential to upset the power balance and reduce his or her authority. A project team does, in fact, create an artificial hierarchy that could compete with the traditional line managers for resources, support, status, talented personnel, and other scarce commodities. However, it is also clear that organizational realities, which mandate the need for project managers and teams, also need to give these individuals authority and status to do their job effectively.

Authority and status, however, typically do not come easily to project managers in most organizations. One way to give project managers a measure of status as part of the formal functional hierarchy is to have them conduct performance appraisals on project team subordinates. On the surface, this suggestion seems to be simple common sense and yet it is often resisted in organizations. Line managers want to maintain control over subordinates through keeping sole right to this evaluation process and, hence, may resist allowing project managers this measure of equal footing. Nevertheless, it is a powerful tool because it sends the clear message throughout the company that projects are valuable and project contributions from team members will be remembered and rewarded [4].

**Learn the fine art of influencing.** How does a project manager succeed in establishing the sort of sustained influence throughout the organization that is useful in the pursuit of project-related goals? An article by Keys and Case [5] highlights five methods managers can use for enhancing their influence with superiors, clients, team members, and other stakeholders. First, they suggest one powerful method for creating a base of influence is to first establish a reputation as an expert in the project that is being undertaken. This finding was also shown in research on project manager influence styles by Thamhain and Gemmill [6]. A project manager who is perceived as lacking any sort of technical skill or competency cannot use influence as a power mechanism to secure the support of other important stakeholders nor be perceived as a true "leader" of the project team. One important caveat to this, however, is that the "expert" label is typically a perceptual one. It may or may not be based in fact. Many of us are aware of project managers who cultivate reputations as technical experts. Unfortunately, in many of these cases, when faced with a true technical problem, the "expertise" they have taken such pains to promote is shown to be woefully inadequate, obsolete or perhaps non-existent. A reputation as an expert is very useful for gaining influence: truly being an expert helps immeasurably with a project manager's credibility.

A second technique for establishing greater influence is to make a distinction between the types of relationships we encounter on the job. Specifically, Keys and Case [5] suggest that managers should make conscious decisions to prioritize their relationships in terms of establishing close ties and contacts with those around the company who will help to accomplish their goals, rather than on the basis of social preference. Certainly, there are personality types and interest groups toward whom each of us are more prone to gravitate. However, to broaden their influence ability, project managers need to break the ties of habit and expand their social networks, particularly with regard to those who can be of future aid.

The third tactic for enhancing influence is networking. As part of creating a wider social set composed of organizational members with the power or status to aid in the project's development, canny project managers will also establish ties to acknowledged experts or those with the ability to provide scarce resources. It is helpful to have experts and resource-providers handy during times of trouble.

A fourth technique for expanding influence is the importance of understanding a key aspect of the influence process: it only works when it is done well. To be influential the project manager must carefully select the right tactic for the situation. For example, many who consider themselves adept at influencing others prefer face-to-face settings rather than using the telephone or leaving messages to request support. They know intuitively that it is harder for others to refuse to offer help when the request is made in person rather than through an impersonal medium. If the tactics selected are not appropriate to the individual and the situation, influence will not work.

Finally, and closely related to the fourth point, successful influencers are socially sensitive, articulate, and flexible. For example, in a face-to-face meeting, a clever influencer knows intuitively how best to balance the alternative methods for attaining the other manager's cooperation and help. The adept influencer can often read the body language and reactions of the "target" manager and may instinctively shift the approach to find the argument most likely to

149

succeed. Whether the approach selected employs pure persuasion, flattery and cajolery, or use of guilt appeals, successful influencers are often those who articulate their arguments well, read nonverbal signals, and tailor their arguments and style to take best advantage of the situation.

**Develop your negotiating skills.** An often neglected aspect of project managers' jobs involves negotiation. They are forced to negotiate daily with a variety of organizational members and external groups. Nevertheless, with the exception of some seasoned project managers who have developed their skills the hard way, through trial and error, most project managers are inherently uncomfortable with the process. Further, because they find it distasteful, they have never sought to actively improve their negotiation skills or learn new techniques and approaches.

**Negotiation is a sometimes distasteful part of the project management process.** All project managers, as part of their understanding of the use of influence in their job, must hone their negotiation skills. As part of this task, learn to recognize the tricks and ploys of those who sit across the table from you. By learning to anticipate and recognize their techniques, it becomes easier to develop appropriate responses. The key is to use a form of negotiation in which you search for fairness [7].Win-win outcomes and mutually acceptable solutions are the guiding principles. A negotiation is not an opportunity to take advantage of the other party. It is a chance to gain the best terms possible, while seeking to address the other party's interests as well. As such, all negotiations should be treated as long-term deals, whether or not this is the case. When we recast a negotiation as a bargaining session between long-time colleagues, it changes the dynamic from one of manipulation and coercion to one of mutual problem-solving.

**Conflict is a natural side effect of project management.** Many managers react to conflict with panic. They view any squabbling among team members as the first step toward team disintegration and ultimate project failure. This response is natural and understandable; after all, it is ultimately your responsibility if the project fails. As a result, the most common reaction to intra-team conflicts is to do everything possible to suppress or minimize the conflict, hoping that if it is ignored it will go away. Unfortunately, it almost never does. Conflict, left to smolder beneath the surface, is a time bomb that will almost always go off at the worst possible time in the development process. If willful ignorance does not work with conflict, what does?

Project managers need to better understand the dynamics of the conflict process and recognize conflict as progress [8]. The natural result of individuals from different functional backgrounds working together is professional tension and personality friction. Suggesting project managers adopt a more sanguine attitude about conflict does not imply that all conflict should be ignored. Nor does it imply that all conflict must be either immediately suppressed or addressed. Instead, it is at the discretion of the project manager how best to handle the problem. Each situation must be dealt with as a unique and separate event. There is no one best method for dealing with conflict, and project managers need to be flexible.

## Summary

Power, politics, and project management are three processes which, while very different, are also inextricably linked. No one can go far in project management without understanding just how far power will take them in their organization. It is in confronting frequent failures at getting their projects successfully implemented through traditional power that most managers are forced, through expedience, to adopt methods for influence and politics. These are not dirty terms, in spite of the fact that the majority of managers in our organizations (1) do not enjoy employing political means to their ends, and (2) do not understand the political processes very well. Too many of us have learned about politics the hard way, through being victimized by someone who was more experienced or more ruthless than we. Given that our first experiences with politics were often unpleasant, it is hardly surprising that many of us "swore off" political behavior, as we would some form of intoxicant.

For better or worse, project managers do not have the luxury of turning their backs on organizational politics. Too much of what they do depends upon their ability to effectively manage not only the technical realms of their job, but the behavioral side as well. Politics constitutes one organizational process that is ubiquitous; it operates across organizations and functional boundaries. Politics is not inherently evil or vicious. Rather, it is only in how it is employed that has earned it so much animus. All of us, bearing the scars of past experiences, understand the potential for misuse that comes from organizational politics.

The purpose of this book has been to shed new light on the twin topics of power and politics, specifically on how they relate to effectively performing the project management function. In doing so, I have taken a concept that has been touched on only peripherally in most project management texts and developed it in greater detail. I hope the readers will take away something from this book that is immediately useful in their project management work. With regard to some of the more predatory practices that fall under the heading of politics, believe in the adage "forewarned is forearmed." This book should give readers a better and more sensitive set of warning signals for spotting and reacting appropriately to unseemly political ploys. Also there is useful information here for novice project managers who are beginning to understand the importance of becoming influential and are eager to learn ways in which to test their wings. May you have a safe and successful flight.

# References

## Chapter 1
1. *A Guide to the Project Management Body of Knowledge.* 1996. Upper Darby, PA: Project Management Institute.
2. Cleland, D. I. and Harold Kerzner. 1985. *A Project Management Dictionary of Terms.* New York: Van Nostrand Reinhold.
3. Bryson, J.M. and P. Bromiley. 1993. Critical factors affecting the planning and implementation of major projects. *Strategic Management Journal,* 14: 319–337.
4. Adams, J.R. and S.E. Barndt. 1988. Behavioral implications of the project life cycle. In *Project Management Handbook,* 2nd Ed., ed. D. I. Cleland and W. R. King, pp. 206–230. New York: Van Nostrand Reinhold.
5. King, William R. and David I. Cleland. 1988. Life cycle management. In *Project Management Handbook,* 2nd Ed., ed. D.I. Cleland and W.R. King, pp. 191–205. New York: Van Nostrand Reinhold.

## Chapter 2
1. Dill, W.R. 1958. Environment as an influence on managerial autonomy. *Administrative Science Quarterly,* 3: 409–443.
2. *A Guide to the Project Management Body of Knowledge.* 1996. Upper Darby, PA: Project Management Institute.
3. Weiner, E. and A. Brown. 1986. Stakeholder analysis for effective issues management. *Planning Review,* 36, 27–31.
4. Mendelow, A. 1986. Stakeholder analysis for strategic planning and implementation. In *Strategic Planning and Management Handbook,* ed. W. R. King and D. I. Cleland, pp. 176–191. New York: Van Nostrand Reinhold.
5. Gaddis, P.O. 1959. The project manager. *Harvard Business Review,* 37: 89–97.
6. Cleland, D.I. 1988. Project stakeholder management. In *Project Management Handbook,* 2nd Ed. D. I. Cleland and W. R. King, pp. 275–301. New York: Van Nostrand Reinhold.
7. Block, R. 1983. *The Politics of Projects.* New York: Yourdon Press.
8. Fisher, R. and W. Ury. 1981. *Getting to Yes: Negotiating Agreement Without Giving In.* New York: Houghton Mifflin.
9. Frame, J.D. 1987. *Managing Projects in Organizations.* San Francisco: Jossey-Bass.
10. Webster, F.M. 1995. Personal communication.

## Chapter 3
1. Webster, F.M. 1995. Personal communication.
2. French, J.R.P. and B. Raven. 1959. "The bases of social power," in D. Cartwright (Ed.), *Studies in Social Power.* Ann Arbor, MI: Institute for Social Research, pp. 150–167.
3. Slevin, D.P. 1989. *The Whole Manager.* New York: AMACOM.
4. May, R. 1972. *Power and Innocence.* New York: Norton.
5. Pinto, J.K. and D.P. Slevin. 1988. "The project champion: key to implementation success," *Project Management Journal,* vol. XX, no. 4, pp. 15–20.

## Chapter 4

1. Butler, A.G. 1973. Project management: A study in organizational conflict. *Academy of Management Journal*, 16: 84–101.

2. Graham, R.J. 1989. *Project Management As If People Mattered*. Bala Cynwyd, PA: Primavera Press.

3. Goodman, R.M. 1967. Ambiguous authority definition in project management. *Academy of Management Journal*, 10: 395–407.

4. Thamhain, H.J. and J.R. Gemmill. 1974. Influence styles of project managers: Some project performance correlates. *Academy of Management Journal*, 17: 216–224.

5. Cialdini, R.B. 1993. *Influence*, 3rd Edition. New York: HarperCollins.

6. Pfeffer, J. 1981. *Power in Organizations*, Marshfield, MA: Pitman.

7. Mintzberg, H. 1983. *Power In and Around Organizations*, Englewood Cliffs, NJ: Prentice-Hall.

8. Mayes, B.T. and R.W. Allen. 1977. Toward a definition of organizational politics. *Academy of Management Review*, 2: 672–678.

9. French, J.R.P. and B. Raven. 1959. The bases of social power, In *Studies in Social Power*, ed. D. Cartwright, pp. 150–167. Ann Arbor, MI: Institute for Social Research.

10. Beeman, D.R. and T.W. Sharkey. 1987. The use and abuse of corporate politics. *Business Horizons*, 36 (2): 26–30.

11. Allen, R.W., D.L. Madison, L.W. Porter, P.A. Renwick, and B.Y. Moyes. 1979. Organizational politics: Tactics and characteristics of actors. *California Management Review*, 22 (1): 77–83.

12. Markus, M.L. 1981. Implementation politics—Top management support and user involvement. *Systems, Objectives, Solutions*, 2: 203–215.

13. Markus, M.L. and J. Pfeffer. 1983. Power and the design and implementation of accounting and control systems. *Accounting, Organizations and Society*, 8: 205–218.

14. March, J.G. and H.A. Simon. 1958. *Organizations*. New York: John Wiley.

15. Lawrence, P.R. and J.W. Lorsch. 1969. *Organization and Environment*, Homewood, IL: Irwin.

16. May, A. 1979. Concorde—Bird of harmony or political albatross? *International Organizations*, Autumn: 481–508.

17. Koenig, C. and R.A. Thietart. 1988. Managers, engineers, and government: The emergence of the mutual organization in the European Aerospace Industry. *Technology in Society*, 10: 45–69.

## Chapter 5

1. Gandz, J. and V.V. Murray. 1980. Experiences of workplace politics. *Academy of Management Journal*, 23: 237–251.

2. Hickson, D.J., C.R. Hinings, C.A. Lee, R.E. Schneck, and J.M. Pennings. 1971. A strategic contingencies theory of intraorganizational power. *Administrative Sciences Quarterly*, 16: 216–229.

3. Harrison, F.L. 1992. *Advanced Project Management: A Structured Approach*. 3rd Ed. New York: Halstead Press.

## Chapter 7

1. Slevin, D.P. 1989. *The Whole Manager.* New York: AMACOM.
2. Maslow, A.H. 1970. *Motivation and Personality,* 2nd Ed. New York: Harper & Row.
3. Alderfer, C.P. 1972. *Existence, Relatedness, and Growth.* New York: Free Press.
4. Fisher, R. and W. Ury. 1981. *Getting to Yes: Negotiating Agreement Without Giving In.* New York: Penguin Books.
5. Matthews, C. 1991. *Hardball: How Politics is Played—Told by One Who Knows the Game.* New York: Summit Books.

## Chapter 8

1. Posner, B.Z. 1986. What's all the fighting about? Conflicts in project management. *IEEE Transactions on Engineering Management,* EM–33: 207–211.
2. Thamhain, H.J. and D.L. Wilemon. 1975. Conflict management in project life cycles. *Sloan Management Review,* 16 (3): 31–50.
3. Thamhain, H.J. and D.L. Wilemon. 1977. Leadership, conflict, and program management effectiveness. *Sloan Management Review,* 19 (1): 69–89.
4. Thomas, K.W. and W.H. Schmidt. 1976. A survey of managerial interests with respect to conflict. *Academy of Management Journal,* 10: 315–318.
5. Thomas, K.W. 1992. Conflict and negotiation processes in organizations, In *Handbook of Industrial and Organizational Psychology,* 2nd Ed., ed. M.D. Dunnette, pp. 889–935. Palo Alto, CA: Consulting Psychologists Press.
6. Pondy, L. 1968. Organizational conflict: Concepts and models. *Administrative Science Quarterly,* 12: 296–320.
7. Ruble, T.L. and K.W. Thomas. 1976. Support for a two-dimensional model of conflict behavior. *Organizational Behavior and Human Performance,* 16,
8. Kilmann, R.H. and K.W. Thomas. 1977. Developing a forced-choice measure of conflict-handling behavior: The MODE instrument. *Educational and Psychological Measurement,* 37: 309–325.
9. Robbins, S.P. 1978. "Conflict management" and "conflict resolution" are not synonymous terms. *California Management Review,* 21 (2): 67–75.
10. Tjosvold, D. 1993. *Teamwork for Customers: Building Organizations that Take Pride in Serving.* San Francisco: Jossey-Bass.
11. McCormack, M.H. 1989. *What They Still Don't Teach You At Harvard Business School.* New York: Bantam Books.
12. Adams, J.R. and S.E. Barndt. 1988. Behavioral implications of the project life cycle, In *Project Management Handbook,* 2nd Ed., ed. D.I. Cleland and W.R. King, pp. 206–230. New York: Van Nostrand Reinhold.
13. Chan, M. 1989. Intergroup conflict and conflict management in the R&D divisions of four aerospace companies. *IEEE Transactions on Engineering Management,* EM–36: 95–104.

## Chapter 9

1. Dill, D.D. and Pearson, A.W. 1984. The effectiveness of project managers: Implications of a political model of influence. *IEEE Transactions on Engineering Management,* EM-31, 138-146.

2. Talbott, G.M. 1994. Advance your career through networking. *Chemical Engineering Progress*, January: 50-53.

3. Lovell, R.J. 1993. Power and the project manager. *International Journal of Project Management*, 11 (2): 73–78.

4. Payne, H.J. 1993. Introducing formal project management into a traditionally structured organization. *International Journal of Project Management*, 11: 239–243.

5. Keys, B. and T. Case. 1990. "How to become an influential manager," *Academy of Management Executive*, IV (4), 38–51.

6. Thamhain, H.J. and J.R. Gemmill. 1974. Influence styles of project managers: Some project performance correlates. *Academy of Management Journal*, 17: 216–224.

7. Fisher, R. and W. Ury. 1981. *Getting to Yes: Negotiating Agreement Without Giving In*. New York: Houghton Mifflin.

8. Pinto, J.K. and O.P. Kharbanda. 1995. *Successful Project Managers: Leading Your Team to Success*. New York: Van Nostrand Reinhold.

# Index

## Suggested Readings

Davis, J.C. 1984. The accidental profession. *Project Management Journal, XV* (3): 6.

Dill, D.D. and A.W. Pearson. 1984. The effectiveness of project managers: Implications of a political model of influence. *IEEE Transactions on Engineering Management,* EM-31, 138-146.

Frame, J. D. 1987. *Managing Projects in Organizations.* San Francisco: Jossey-Bass.

Graham, R.J. 1992. A survival guide for the accidental project manager. *Proceedings of the Annual Project Management Institute Symposium,* Drexel Hill, PA: Project Management Institute, 355-361.

Lawrence, P.R. and J.W. Lorsch. 1967. Differentiation and integration in complex organizations. *Administrative Science Quarterly,* 11: 1-47.

Lovell, R.J. 1993. Power and the project manager. *International Journal of Project Management,* 11 (2): 73-78.

Lord, M.A. 1993. Implementing strategy through project management. *Long Range Planning,* 26: 76-88.

Madison, D.L., R.W. Allen, L.W. Porter, P.A. Renwick, and B.T. Mayes. 1980. Organizational politics: An exploration of manager's perceptions. *Human Relations,* 33: 74-100.

Markus, M.L. 1983. Power, politics, and MIS implementation. *Communications of the ACM,* 26: 430-444.

McCormack, M.H. 1989. *What They Still Don't Teach You in Harvard Business School.* New York: Bantam.

Payne, H.J. 1993. Introducing formal project management into a traditionally structured organization. *International Journal of Project Management,* 11: 239-243.

Randolph, W.A. and B.Z. Posner. 1989. What every manager should know about project management. *Sloan Management Review,* 29 (4): 65-73.

Salancik, G.R. and J. Pfeffer. 1989. "Who gets power—And how they hold on to it: A strategic-contingency model of power," in H.J. Leavitt, L.R. Pondy, and D.M. Boje (Eds.), *Readings in Managerial Psychology,* 4th Ed. Chicago: University of Chicago Press, pp. 346-366.

Talbott, G.M. 1994. Advance your career through networking. *Chemical Engineering Progress,* January: 50-53.

Thamhain, H.J. 1991. Developing project management skills. *Project Management Journal,* XXII (3): 39-53.

Wheelen, T.L. and J.D. Hunger. 1992. *Strategic Management and Business Policy,* 4th Ed. Reading, MA: Addison-Wesley.

## Other books published by Project Management Institute

*Achieving TQM on Projects: The Journey of Continuous Improvement*
Russell W. Darnall
120pp, 1994, $22.95, hardcover, ISBN:1-880410-35-4

*Successful Information Systems Implementation: The Human Side*
Jeffrey K. Pinto
220pp, 1994, $16.95, paperback, ISBN: 1-880410-37-0

The Human Aspects of Project Management:

*Organizing Projects for Success* (Volume One)
Vijay K. Verma
201pp., 1995, $24.95, paperback, ISBN: 1-880410-40-0

*Human Resource Skills for the Project Manager* (Volume Two)
Vijay K. Verma
1995, $24.95, paperback, ISBN: 1-880410-41-9

*Managing the Project Team* (Volume Three)
Vijay K. Verma
1996, $19.95, paperback, ISBN: 1-880410-42-7

*A Guide to the Project Management Body of Knowledge*
*(PMBOK Guide)*
The PMI Standards Committee
1996, $29.95, hardcover, ISBN: 1-880410-13-3
1996, $10.00, paperback, ISBN: 1-880410-12-5

*The Global Status of the Project Management Profession*
1996, $35.95, paperback, ISBN: 1-880410-34-6

*Decision Analysis in Projects*
John R. Schuyler
1996, $24.95, paperback, ISBN: 1-880410-39-7

*Earned Value Project Management Systems*
Quentin W. Fleming and Joel M. Koppelman
1996, $24.95, paperback, ISBN: 1-880410-38-9